Instant Pot Pressure Cooker Cookbook

Over 100 Delicious Pressure Cooker Recipes For
The Whole Family

RONNIE ISRAEL

ISBN-13:978-1517507312

ISBN-10:1517507316

DEDICATION

To all those who love to cook

TABLE OF CONTENTS

Other Books By Ronnie Israel

Electric Pressure Cooker Recipes: Over 100 Delicious Quick And Easy Recipes For Fast Meals

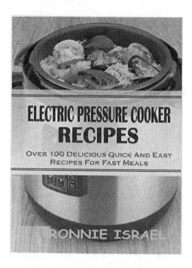

The Wok Cookbook: Delicious And Filling Chinese Recipes To Enjoy

INTRODUCTION

I want to thank you for downloading this book. And if you just bought an Instant Pot programmable pressure cooker; congratulations! You have a new best friend that will make cooking times a fast and delightful experience for you. Your food will taste heavenly and your friends and family will love you more. Additionally, you now have the time to engage in that new activity that you have been longing to try. With your Instant pot, you will definitely enjoy quick, safe, convenient, dependable and sophisticated cooking.

The Instant Pot is an intelligent multi-cooker. Once you have it, you no longer need a slow cooker, stove pressure cooker, steamer, yogurt maker, rice cooker/porridge maker, stockpot warmer and sauté/browning pan. With just a push of a button, you will find yourself performing lots of perfect 'magic food tricks' like stewing, braising and slow cooking. It is 2 to 6 times faster than regular coking and uses up to70% less energy. Instant

Pot is specifically designed for those who lead a fast-paced, health-oriented life style. It produces perfect, healthy and nutritious meals conveniently and at all times.

Pressure cooking is more than one-pot cooking. While you can cook an entire meal like your sauces and stews in it, a pressure cooker instant pot is also a great aid to daily cooking. For instance, you can pressure cook ribs and then transfer on the BBQ. They really help to safely speed up the cooking process. Most importantly, they help to cook foods faster with less energy while retaining more nutrients. Pressure cooking in your Instant Pot is really a great way to cook meat, stews, soups, rice, beans, potatoes, breakfasts, desserts, and just about anything else.

The Benefits Of Instant Pot

Here are a few benefits of using an instant pot pressure cooker:

Convenience

It has 12 turn-key function keys to aid the most common cooking tasks. It has the benefit of delayed cooking for up to 24 hours so you can effectively plan your meals. It helps to reduce cooking time as well.

Cooks Healthy Nutritious And Tasty Meals

Pressure cooking is healthy cooking. With its extra speed and heat higher temperature cooking, it preserves natural nutrients and vitamins. Studies show that it preserves up to 90-95% of the vitamins in vegetables. Boiling helps to retain about 40-75%, while conventional steaming retains about 75-90%! The flavors and colors of foods are also retained, giving you the best that foods have to offer. The Instant Pot with its smart programming feature produces delicious healthy foods, every time.

2

Clean & Pleasant

The instant pot, as with all other pressure cookers, contains splatters effectively. So no more splatters on your stove top or spillovers in the oven. Additionally, it is totally quiet, and produces no steam, smells or excessive kitchen heat.

Fast And Easy

The Instant Pot cooks at a higher temperature than conventional cooking. Its use of more heat means more speed and faster cooking, reducing cooking time up to 70%. Simply push a few buttons and cook your entire meal in just a few steps. It is as easy as ABC!

Green Cooking and Energy Efficient

Save up to 70% of energy/ electricity by cooking in your Instant pot. Less heat and less time means this very high percentage of energy savings over other types of cooking.

Absolutely Safe And Dependable

The Instant Pot has 10 fool-proof safety protections. It's so fool-proof that even if one fails, another will immediately take its place. Its safety features are so well built- in, the lid will not unlock if there is still some pressure in the cooker. They are absolutely safe and dependable.

Cooking Methods

<u>Braising</u>

The aim of braising meats and vegetables is to make them juicer and more tender. This cooking method uses low heat to break down the tough connective tissue in less expensive cuts of meat. Braising often starts by browning meat in a small amount of oil. Press the sauté function in your Instant pot to brown the meat in a small amount of heated oil. Cover the meat with a small amount of liquid and deglaze the pan. Add other ingredients, press the stew/ meat function and cook at a low temperature. The cooking environment in your instant pot significantly reduces the braising time needed. It takes only 45 to 60 minutes to braise a roast in the pressure cooker while it will take up to 3 hours to do the same in a stove or oven.

<u>Deglazing</u>

Deglazing is simply the process of removing excess fat or fragments that may be left in the pan. It involves heating the pan and adding some cooking liquid to enable you scrape up any browned bits that are stuck to the bottom. When you deglaze before adding other ingredients for your soups or sauce, it comes out with more color and flavor.

<u>Sautéing</u>

Sautéing involves cooking food quickly and lightly in a few spoons of oil, butter or fat. A sauté pan is brought to temperature over medium-high heat, and then thin or small pieces of food, such as onions and garlic, are quickly added and sautéed to bring out their delightful aroma. In your instant pot, you only need to press the sauté button and this will brown the surface of the food to increase its delicious flavors and aromas

Steaming

In steaming, the steam from the cooking liquid is used to cook the food. Steaming usually starts when water is added to the pan, a rack or tray is also added and the food is then placed on top of this rack or tray. The water heats and the resulting steam heats the food. Steaming is perfect for vegetables, they become tender when steamed but still retain their nutrients and color

Pressure Cooking

Pressure cooking involves using the steam that is sealed in a pressure cooker, a special airtight cooking pot, to cook food. The sealed liquid such as broth, water or wine, traps the steam that rises from the liquid, raising the pressure inside the pressure cooker and the maximum temperature of the liquid. Consequently, the cooking process is quickened. Pressure cooking helps to retain moisture in foods, which results in more concentrated flavors. It also helps to retain more nutrients and vitamins in your food.

Rice Cooker

The Instant Pot's rice cooker function is just great! Simply add the rice and water, secure the lid and press the button. 30 to 40 minutes later, you have a delicious and fluffy rice meal to enjoy. There is no need to bother about remembering to stir or to constantly check to prevent burning. You only need to remember this simple formula for cooking different types of rice:

For white rice, use 1 cup water per 1 cook rice.

For wild rice or brown rice, use 11/2 cups of water per 1 cup rice. For extra flavor, you could try using chicken or vegetable broth instead of water.

<u>Slow Cooker</u>

Slow cooking is a "set and forget" cooking method. Simply put something up the morning and by evening, you have a great meal waiting for you. Slow cooking is perfect for soups, stews and meats.

Three Methods Of Opening The Cooker

There are three methods or ways of opening your instant pot after every cooking.

<u>Quick Release</u> - this method releases pressure instantly. Simply press [Cancel] and then twist the steam release handle on the lid to the "Venting" position.

<u>Natural Release</u> - this method continues to cook the food using the heat and steam that is left in the cooker. Simply press [Cancel] and wait for the pressure to come down naturally and the lid to unlock. This usually takes about 20 minutes but if the cooker is very full, it could take more.

<u>10-minute Natural Release</u> – this method automatically takes the cooker to the "Keep Warm" mode and begins to count 10 minutes. Simply press [Cancel] and then twist the steam release handle on the lid to the "Venting" position.

BREAKFAST & BRUNCH RECIPES

Fruity Irish Oatmeal

For different flavors, you could try using other dried fruits such as cherries, prunes and dates. You can also add butter to this meal for extra flavor and to prevent the oatmeal from foaming. Note that foaming can clog the pressure release valve.

Fruity Irish Oatmeal can also be made the night before. Once cooled, place it in two microwave-safe containers, cover and chill overnight. The next morning, cover each container with a paper towel to prevent splatters and then heated until through.

Servings: 2

Ingredients

1 cup toasted steel-cut oats

1 cup apple juice

2 teaspoons butter

1 tablespoon of dried cranberries

1 tablespoon snipped dried apricots

1 tablespoon golden raisins

¼ teaspoon ground cinnamon

1 tablespoon of maple syrup

Chopped toasted walnuts or pecans, optional

Maple syrup or brown sugar, optional

Heavy cream, milk or half-and-half, optional

3 cups water

Pinch salt

Directions

1. Place the rack in the Instant Pot and pour ½ cup of water over it.

2. Combine thoroughly 2½ cups of water, oats, apple juice, butter, apricots, cinnamon, raisins, cranberries, maple syrup and salt in a heat-proof bowl and fit it inside the Instant Pot to rest on the rack.

3. Seal lid and select the manual mode. For chewy oatmeal, cook for 5 minutes and for creamy oatmeal, cook for 8 minutes.

4. Remove from the heat. Let the pressure release naturally. Gently lift the metal bowl out of your Instant pot with tongs.

5. Spoon oats into bowls. Serve topped with more maple syrup or brown sugar, nuts and heavy cream, milk or half-and half.

Scrambled Sausage And Cheese

You may use your favorite cheese for this recipe.

Servings: 8

Ingredients

1 pound ground sausage

1 1-pound bag frozen hash browns, thawed

8 large eggs

1 tablespoon vegetable or olive oil

1 green bell pepper, seeded & diced

1 red bell pepper, seeded & diced

1 large sweet onion, diced

1 yellow or orange bell pepper, seeded & diced

¼ cup heavy cream or water

½ pound Cheddar cheese, grated

Salt &freshly ground pepper, to taste

A few drops hot sauce, optional

Directions

1. Add the oil to the Instant Pot and bring to medium-high heat.

2. Add the onion and bell peppers and sauté about 5 minutes. Add the hash browns and sausage, stir and cook 10 minutes on low pressure.

3. Remove from the heat, quick-release the pressure and remove lid. Drain any excess fat and discard.

4. Return to medium heat. Whisk eggs, heavy cream or water, salt, pepper and hot sauce, if using, and pour over the sausage-potato mixture. Stir and scramble the eggs until they start to set.

5. Top with cheese, cover the instant pot, and cook for 1-2 minutes until cheese melts. Serve with biscuits or toasted whole grain bread spread with honey-butter.

Quick Oats Breakfast

A quick and delicious breakfast that leaves no mess in the pot.

Cook Time: 10 minutes

Servings: 3-4

Ingredients

1 cup oats, steel cut

2 cups water

Milk and or cream

Pinch salt

Sugar, optional

Directions

1. Add 1 cup water into the inner pot of the Instant Pot and place trivet in pot.

2. Put the oats, water and salt in a heat proof bowl and place it in the inner pot on trivet. Secure lid.

3. Manual cook for 7-8 minutes and quick release steam. While the oats are cooking, heat the milk.

4. Once oats are cooked, remove from inner pot and serve. Pour milk on top, cream and sugar if using.

Egg Muffins Delight
Servings: 4

Ingredients

4 eggs

4 tablespoon cheddar/Jack cheese, shredded

4 slices precooked bacon, crumbled

1 green onion, diced

1/4 tsp lemon pepper seasoning

1 ½ cups of water

Directions

1. Place a trivet in the bottom of Instant Pot and add water.

2. Add together the eggs and lemon pepper in a large bowl and beat well.

3. Grease 4 small ramekins lightly with olive oil. Divide the bacon, cheese and green onion evenly into the ramekins.

4. Pour the eggs into the ramekins, stirring gently. Place the ramekins on the trivet and cook8 minutes on high pressure

5. Quick- release pressure and serve.

Breakfast Quinoa In The Instant Pot

A perfect and healthy way to start your day is to take this light and fluffy quinoa, served with sliced almonds and fresh berries. Also, it takes just 1 minute to prepare in your Instant Pot.

Servings: 6

Ingredients

1 1/2 cups uncooked quinoa

1/4 teaspoon ground cinnamon

2 tablespoons of maple syrup

1/2 teaspoon vanilla

2 1/4 cups of water

A pinch of salt

Milk, fresh berries and sliced almonds, for toppings

Directions

1. Rinse the quinoa well then add it to the Instant Pot together with water, vanilla, maple syrup, cinnamon, and salt.

2. Manual cook for 1 minute on high pressure. When done, wait for10 minutes, and then quick release pressure.

3. When valve drops, remove lid carefully.

4. Fluff the quinoa. Enjoy hot with milk, sliced almonds and berries.

Homemade Applesauce

This delicious homemade applesauce goes well on steel cut oatmeal. It can also be taken as a snack.

Servings: 12

Ingredients

3 lbs. apples, peeled, cored& quartered

¾ teaspoon of ground cinnamon

1/3 cup of apple juice, unsweetened

Directions

1. Combine all ingredients in the Instant Pot. Cook for 1 minute on high.

2. Let the pressure release slowly. Serve warm or cold.

Apple Buckwheat Cobbler
Ingredients

3- 3.5 lbs. raw apples, cut into chunks

½ cup medjool dates, chopped

½ cup dry buckwheat

2 teaspoon cinnamon

¼ tsp nutmeg

1 ½ cups of water

¼ teaspoon of powdered ginger

Directions

1. Put all the ingredients in the Instant Pot, stirring well to mix.

13

2. Cook for 12 minutes on medium pressure. Serve warm or cold.

Apple & Cherry Breakfast Risotto

Delicious, creamy and nutritious, this breakfast recipe is also quick and easy to prepare.

Servings: 4

Ingredients

1 1/2 cups Arborio rice

2 tablespoon of butter

2 large apples, cored & diced

1/3 cup brown sugar

1 1/2 tsp cinnamon

1 cup apple juice

1/2 cup dried cherries

3 cups milk

1/4 tsp salt

Directions

1. Melt the butter using the sauté mode. Add the rice, cook for 3 to 4 minutes, stirring constantly.

2. Add the apples, brown sugar, spices, juice and milk and then stir. Cook 6 minutes on high pressure

3. Using the quick release, remove rice from the cooker and stir in the cherries gently.

4. Serve hot, topped with almonds and milk.

Sunrise Sandwiches

Servings: 2

Ingredients

4 slices of rye bread

2 thin slices prosciutto or meat

2 eggs

2 tablespoon of cheddar cheese, grated

Drop of olive oil

2 cups water

Directions

1. Place a trivet in the bottom of the pressure cooker and add water.

2. Grease the bottom of two ramekins lightly with olive oil and line it with the prosciutto slices. Add egg (scrambled or whole) on top.

3. Add pepper and cheese on top. Cover ramekins with foil, place it in a steamer basket and place the steamer basket on top of the trivet.

4. Cook 6 minutes on low pressure. Let the pressure decrease slowly. In the interim, toast the bread and butter it, if desired.

5. Remove the ramekins from the cooker and use a knife to loosen the edge.

6. Pour out the egg & meat mixture onto the bread slices. Serve immediately.

Blueberry Croissant Pudding

Perfect for a brunch, this recipe comes with a fresh delightful twist.

Servings: 10

Ingredients

1 cup blueberries, fresh or frozen

3 large croissants, cut (5 to 5 1/2 cups)

1- 8-ounce cream cheese, softened

2 eggs

2/3 cup sugar

1 cup of milk

1 teaspoon of vanilla

Directions

1. Place the croissants in a heat- proof bowl and add the blueberries.

2. Whisk together the eggs, cream cheese, vanilla and sugar in a bowl until well mixed. Add the milk and mix thoroughly.

3. Pour the egg mixture over the croissants and then let it sit 20 minutes. Cook 20 minutes on high pressure.

4. Let the pressure release slowly. Serve topped with powdered sugar.

Cinnamon Bread Pudding With Caramel Sauce

A bread pudding that is just perfect for breakfast.

Servings: 8

Ingredients

7 thick slices of cinnamon bread, cubed & toasted

4 tablespoons of butter, melted

3 cups whole milk

½ cup of packed brown sugar

1 tsp vanilla extract

¼ tsp salt

3 eggs, beaten

½ cup raisins

¾ cup brown sugar

¼ cup of corn syrup

1 tsp ground cinnamon

2 tablespoons heavy cream

2 tablespoons butter

½ teaspoon salt

1 teaspoon vanilla extract

½ cup pecans, toasted & chopped

Caramel pecan sauce, optional

1½ cups water

Directions

1. Combine the eggs, butter, vanilla, brown sugar, cinnamon, milk and salt and whisk well. Add the raisins and the bread. Let this mixture rest 20 minutes before cooking to absorb well but stir occasionally.

2. After 20 minutes, pour the mixture into a metal or glass baking dish and cover this dish with foil. Using a long piece of foil, make a handle to lift out the dish.

3. Add water to the Instant Pot and place a trivet in the bottom. Now, place the baking dish on top and cook 20 minutes on high pressure. Quick-release pressure.

 4. Meanwhile, prepare the caramel sauce by combining the cream, butter, syrup, sugar and salt in a saucepan. Set on medium heat and bring to a boil, stirring frequently.

5. When the mixture boils, lower heat and keep cooking until the sugar dissolves completely. Add the nuts and vanilla. Serve caramel sauce on top of the bread pudding.

POULTRY RECIPES

Chicken &Tomatillo Sauce

Enjoy this mild but savory dish.

Prep Time: 10 minutes

Cook Time: 15 minutes

Servings: 4-6

Ingredients:

1-2 tablespoon of olive oil

1 large onion sliced

1 teaspoon garlic powder or 1 clove garlic, crushed

2lb boneless/skinless chicken thighs

14 oz tomatillos or salsa verde

1 can green chilies (127 ml)

Salt and pepper, to taste

1 tsp ground coriander or1 handful fresh cilantro

¾ cups garbanzo beans

3 cups cheddar cheese

1 ¾ cups of leftover rice

½ cup black olives

¾ cups chopped tomatoes

Directions

1. In your Instant Pot, sauté onions in oil until translucent. Sauté garlic for 15 seconds and add the chicken, chilies, cilantro, tomatillos, salt and pepper to taste.

2. Select the "Poultry" option and 8 minutes cooking time, "keep- warm" for 3 minutes and then release pressure.

3. Remove the chicken and break it up with two forks. Add rice and garbanzo beans and sauté 1 minute. Put the meat back to the Instant Pot to reheat. Add the cheese and stir.

4. Serve with refried beans salad and tortillas. It can be used as a burrito filling as well.

No- Water Salt Baked Chicken

This recipe is just right for parties. Your guests and family will forever remember this flavorsome and tasty dish.

Prep Time: 15 minutes

Cook Time: 60 minutes

Servings: 8

Ingredients:

1 medium size chicken

1 small ginger piece, minced

1 green onion, minced

2 tablespoons of sugar

2 teaspoons of soy sauce

2 teaspoons of salt

2 tablespoons wine or 1 tablespoon cooking wine

Directions

1. Combine the salt and sugar and season the chicken, (inside and outside) well.

2. Sprinkle 1 tsp of salt in the bottom of the inner pot and place the seasoned chicken, wine and soy sauce into the Instant Pot.

3. Select the "Poultry" button. Once done, turn the chicken over and then select the "Poultry" button again.

4. Cut the chicken into pieces, serve and enjoy with a dipping sauce. To make this sauce, simply combine green onion and ginger with the chicken oil.

Duck And Veggies

After a hard day's work, you will enjoy this delicious duck cooked with vegetables.

Prep Time: 15 minutes

Cook Time: 40 minutes

Servings: 8

Ingredients

1 cucumber cut into pieces

1 medium size duck

2 carrots cut into pieces

2 tablespoons wine or 1 tablespoon cooking wine

1 small ginger, cut into pieces

2 teaspoons of salt

2 cups of water

Directions

1. Put all the ingredients in the Instant Pot; press the Meat/Stew button.

2. Once done, serve and enjoy.

Ligurian Sea Lemon Chicken

Servings: 4-6

Ingredients

4 Lemons, three juiced and one for garnish

3 fresh rosemary sprigs (two for chopping, one for garnish)

1 chicken, cut into 8 parts

2 garlic cloves

1/2 bunch parsley leaves and stems

2 sprigs of fresh sage

4 Tbsp Extra Virgin Olive Oil

1/2 cup of dry white wine

1 cup stock or water

4ounces black gourmet salt-cured olives (kalamata, taggiesche or French)

Salt and pepper

Directions

1. For the marinade, chop together the rosemary, garlic, parsley and sage. Place them all in a bowl and add the olive oil, lemon juice, salt and pepper. Combine and set aside.

2. Place the chicken in a bowl and cover with the marinade. Cover with plastic wrap, and let it marinate for 2-4 hours in the refrigerator.

3. Pre-heat cooker by pressing sauté. Add olive oil and brown the chicken pieces about 5 minutes on all sides. De-glaze the pressure cooker with the wine for about 3 minutes until nearly evaporated.

4. Return the chicken piece to the pot in their right order: dark meat such as legs, wings and thighs first and then chicken breast on top, without touching the bottom of the pot.

5. Pour in the remaining marinade and stock over them. Lock lid into place, press the manual button and choose 12 minutes of pressure cooking time.

6. Quick release by pressing cancel and twisting the steam release handle on the lid to the venting position.

7. Remove chicken pieces and place in a serving bowl. Press sauté to reduce the liquid in the pot to 1/4 of its amount and then pour over chicken.

8. Serve with fresh lemon slices, fresh rosemary and olives.

Chicken & Rice Pudding
Servings: 6–8

<u>Ingredients:</u>

12 chicken thighs, boneless, skinless

<u>Marinade:</u>

2 tablespoons of fresh lime juice

¼ cup olive oil

1 tablespoon of sea salt

3 cloves garlic, roughly chopped

½ teaspoon black pepper, freshly ground

1 tablespoon oregano, dried or 3 tablespoons oregano, fresh minced

2 teaspoons of ground cumin

<u>Sofrito:</u>

½ medium green bell pepper, seeded& coarsely chopped

½ medium yellow onion, coarsely chopped

3 – 4 cloves garlic

1 large handful cilantro

¼ teaspoon fresh ground black pepper

½ teaspoon sea salt

24

Rice:

2 tablespoons of coconut oil

1 medium red bell pepper, seeded & small diced

1 medium yellow onion, small diced

1 teaspoon ground cumin

1 teaspoon dried oregano or 1 tablespoon minced fresh oregano

28 ounce can Muir Glen Organic Fire Roasted Diced Tomatoes, liquid inclusive

5 cups organic chicken stock

3 cups long grain brown rice

1 ½ cups Spanish olive

¼ teaspoon sea salt

2 tablespoons of olive brine

Directions

Marinade

1. Combine olive oil, garlic, sea salt, pepper, oregano, cumin and lime in a large non-reactive bowl or Ziploc bag. Add the chicken and coat evenly with the marinade. Let marinade sit for at least one hour or overnight. Stir occasionally.

Sofrito

2. In a food processor, add together, green bell pepper, onion, garlic, cilantro, sea salt and pepper and process until smooth.

Rice

3. Select the "Sauté" function on your Instant Pot and melt coconut oil. Take out the chicken from the marinade, reserve any leftovers.

4. Brown the chicken in batches per side for4- 5 minutes, until golden brown. Remove chicken to a platter and set aside.

5. Add onion, cumin, oregano and red bell pepper, sautéing about 5 minutes until just tender.

6. Add the sofrito, stir and sauté 3 minutes. Add the stock, leftover marinade, if any, diced tomatoes, and sea salt, simmering for about 2 minutes.

7. Stir in the rice, brine and olives and add the browned chicken pieces to it. Secure lid on the Instant Pot, press the Meat/Stew button and set timer to15 minutes.

8. Once done, allow the pressure to release naturally, remove lid and serve.

Steamed Chicken With Traditional Chinese Garlic Sauce

A well- loved popular traditional Chinese dish

Prep Time: 30 minutes

Cook Time: 12 minutes

Servings: 6

Ingredients

9 pieces Chicken drumsticks (about 2 .2lb)

1 tablespoon olive oil

2 tablespoon freshly minced garlic

1 tablespoon Chinese salted fermented soya beans (minced &black colored)

1 tablespoon green onion, freshly chopped

<u>For Marinade</u>

1 tablespoon Kikkoman light soy sauce

1 tablespoon dark soy sauce

2/3 teaspoon salt

11/2 tablespoon corn starch

2 tablespoon water

Directions

1. Begin by cleaning the chicken drumsticks, removing the bones and then cutting them into pieces. Mix all the marinade ingredients together, add drumsticks. Refrigerate overnight in a lidded container.

2. Heat olive oil in a small sauté pan over medium-high heat. Add the minced Chinese salted fermented soya beans and garlic. Cook 1 minute and add to a bowl, setting aside. Now mix thoroughly with the marinated chicken.

3 Add 2 cups water in pressure cooker, place the steam rack into the cooker and place the bowl with the chicken on the rack. Cover lid, checking that the valve is set to 'seal. Press the "steam" function and set the cooking time for 12 minutes.

4: When done, wait 5 minutes, release pressure and open the lid. Remove the bowl. Add green onion, mix and serve.

Under Vacuum Duck Breast

In the 1960s and 70s, French chefs sealed foods in plastic bags and cooked them at a low and constant temperatures for an extended period of time. This food cooking technique produces higher succulence and prevents overcooking. For these reasons, it became popular at gourmet restaurants. Now, you can use your instant pot pressure cooker to produce the same effect.

Prep Time: 10 Minutes

Cook Time: 38+4 Minutes

Servings: 2

Ingredients

2 large boneless duck breast, halves, 1.1 lb, with skin-on

1 teaspoon salt

½ teaspoon black pepper, freshly ground

2 teaspoons garlic, freshly minced

1/3 teaspoon peppercorn

1/3 teaspoon dry thyme

1 tablespoon of vegetable oil

1 large ripe apricot, peeled, cored& mashed with 2 tbsp of water

2 teaspoons sugar

Apricot sauce (optional)

Directions

1. Clean duck breasts, mix together all the ingredients and rub on duck breasts.

2. Cover and refrigerate 2 hours. Rinse off the spices and place the duck breasts in a Ziploc bag and seal.

3. Add water to pressure cooker; cook up to the 7-cup mark. Open lid, turn power on and press the 'Keep warm' button. After 20 minutes, place Ziploc bag in water bath for 35 to 40 minutes.

4. Remove bag from water and pat dry the duck breasts. Add 1 tablespoon vegetable oil to a skillet and sear duck breasts at medium-high heat until golden. Turn over to the other skin side and cook for 20 seconds more.

5: Slice duck breasts and enjoy with apricot sauce.

6. To make the sauce, mix the apricot, which has been mashed with water, add the sugar and place in a small pot. Bring to boil on high heat and then simmer at low heat for 5 minutes.

Tender Chicken Potato Rice

Quick, easy and flavorful, this yummy recipe is a blend of goodies. With its tender chicken meat, flavorful rice and powdery potato, you will definitely agree!

Prep Time: 15 minutes

Cook time: 40 minutes

Servings: 8

Ingredients

Boneless and skinless chicken thighs (1 lb) cut to small pieces

1 small piece of fresh ginger sliced

1 1/3cups white long rice

2 tablespoon of olive oil

1 green onion cut in 2-inch length

1 star anise

3 cloves

2cups chicken stock or water

1 tablespoon Kikkoman light soy sauce

11/2 tablespoon dark soy sauce

1/2 teaspoon salt

3 medium yellow potatoes peeled & cut in ¼ inch pieces

1 finely chopped green onion

1 tablespoon sesame oil

For Marinade

¼ teaspoon white pepper powder

1 tablespoon dark soy sauce

1 tablespoon Kikkoman light soy sauce

1 tablespoon corn starch

2 tablespoon water

Directions

1. Combine chicken and all marinade ingredients together. Do this the night before. Seal in a container and place in the fridge overnight.

2. Heat olive oil over medium-high heat in a sauté pan. Add onions, anise and ginger and cook 1minute. Add marinated chicken, stir often for 3 to 4 minutes until light brown.

3. Transfer cooked chicken, liquid inclusive, into the Instant Pot. Add water or chicken stock, rice, peeled potatoes, dark soy sauce, Kikkoman light soy sauce and salt. Cook 35 minutes.

4. When done, wait 10 minutes more and then release pressure; open the lid. Add green onion and sesame oil. Cover and sit rice for 5 minutes. Serve and enjoy!

Instant Pot Turkey Chili

A delicious chili you can't resist!

Cook Time: 10 minutes

Servings: 4

Ingredients:

1 lb lean ground turkey

15 ounces chick peas (previously cooked)

1 yellow bell pepper, diced

I medium onion, diced

2 – 3 cloves garlic, peeled

21/2 tablespoons of chili powder

11/2 teaspoon cumin

1/8 teaspoon cayenne

2 cans original rotel

4-5 ounces water

1 –5.5 ounces can V8

12-ounces vegetable stock or12 ounces water with vegetable stock

Directions

1. Add the ground turkey and water to Instant Pot. Select the manual function, secure the pressure valve and set 5-minutes cooking time.

2. Once done, allow 5-10 minutes of rest, release pressure and open the lid.

3. Break up the ground turkey and add the rest of the ingredients, select the manual function and set cooking time for 5minutes.

4. Once done, allow 5-10 minutes of rest, release pressure and open the lid. Stir and serve.

Steamed Duck With Potato

Enjoy a no-splatter-on the stove-and-wall cooking with your Instant Pot when you are preparing this delicious braised duck.

Ingredients

1 Potato, cut into cubes

1 Whole duck, cut into chunks

4 garlic cloves

2 green onions, cut into length of 2 inches

1 (1 inch) piece fresh ginger root, sliced

4 table spoons of rice/sherry wine

4 table spoons of sugar

4 table spoons of soy sauce

1/2 teaspoons of salt

1/4 cup of water

Directions

1. Press "Sauté" to heat up the Instant Pot for 1 minute.

2. Place the chopped duck, skin side down, in the instant pot and sear until golden brown.

3. Stir all ingredients in, except the potato, and press the poultry setting.

4. When done, release pressure, open the lid and add the potato cubes, stir and press "manual" for 5 minute.

5. Serve and enjoy.

Braised Turkey Thighs In The Instant Pot

Instead of the Poultry setting, the slow-cooker setting can also be used for this yummy turkey dish. Simply set your Instant Pot to slow cook for 4 hours.

Servings: 4

<u>Ingredients</u>

2 turkey thighs (about 1 lb), trimmed of excess fat

1 cup chicken broth

1 tbsp red-wine vinegar

1 cup onions, thinly sliced

1 cup Portobello mushrooms, sliced

2 tsp minced garlic

½ tsp dried rosemary

½ tsp thyme

½ tsp sage

½ tsp salt and pepper

<u>Gravy:</u>

¼ cup water

3 tbsp flour

Directions

1. Set the Instant-Pot to Sauté and brown turkey thighs. Add all other ingredients, close lid, press the Poultry setting and cook 1 hour.

2. Quick release; check for doneness and if undone, cook another15 minutes on Poultry setting.

3. Once meat is done, remove to cutting board and cover with foil.

4. To make gravy, whisk flour and water in a small bowl until thoroughly blended. Add the flour mixture into onions, liquid and mushrooms in the pressure cooker, mixing well.

5. Set to Keep-warm and simmer the gravy until thickened, for 15 minutes.

6. Arrange on 4 serving plates and spoon on some gravy.

Chicken With Bing Cherries & Wild Rice
Servings: 4-8

Ingredients

Chicken:

12 chicken thighs

1 orange peeled& quartered

4 sprigs of rosemary

1 cup Balsamic vinegar

½ cup of evaporated palm sugar

¼ cup of melted butter

1 tablespoon molasses

1 onion, julienned

1 1/2 cups pitted & halved fresh Bing Cherries

¼ teaspoon of sea salt

Wild Rice:

1 1/3 cups wild rice, rinsed

1 onion, minced

¼ cup butter

2 plum tomatoes, diced

4 cups low sodium vegetable stock

1/2 cup pitted & halved fresh Bing cherries

½ cup toasted pumpkin seeds

Sea salt to taste

Directions

1. Add the evaporated palm sugar, balsamic vinegar, molasses, orange, onion and butter to the Instant Pot, mixing well. Add the chicken, rosemary and salt, stirring to coat.

2. Add the cherries. Secure lid on the Instant Pot. Press the Meat/Stew button and adjust time to 25 minutes.

3. When done, allow the pressure to release naturally and remove the lid.

4. While the chicken is cooking, add the vegetable stock to a medium saucepan on the stove top and bring to a boil. Add the wild rice. Cover and simmer 50 minutes.

5. Heat butter in a large pan. Sauté the onion until caramelized. Add tomato and sauté 3 to 4 minutes. Add tomato and onions to the rice.

6. Add cherries to the pan and sauté until soft and juicy, for 3 to 4 minutes. Add toasted pumpkin seeds and cherries, stirring to incorporate. Add salt to taste.

7. Place the wild rice on a platter and top with chicken. Pour the chicken juices over the platter and garnish dish with rosemary.

Balsamic& Garlic Chicken Thighs

If you are serving this tender and delicious meal with Jasmine rice, cook the rice first. When cooking, add some pats of butter to the rice.

Servings: 4

Ingredients:

1 lb of Boneless, Skinless Chicken thighs – about 8pieces

1-1/2 teaspoons of minced garlic

2 tablespoons of fresh cilantro, chopped

1 teaspoon dried basil

2 tablespoons green onion, minced

1 teaspoon garlic powder

2 tablespoons light olive oil

1/2 cup of Balsamic Vinegar

1 teaspoon Worcestershire sauce

1/3 cup cream Sherry wine

1/2 teaspoon salt

1/2 teaspoon Pepper

Directions

1. Combine Worcestershire sauce, balsamic vinegar, garlic powder, minced onion, basil, Sherry, salt and pepper in a plastic bag. Mix thoroughly.

2. To this mixture, add the chicken, ensuring the chicken is covered in this sauce and set aside.

3. Select the sauté option in your Instant Pot, add the olive oil and sauté the garlic, stirring often.

4. Select the Poultry option, add the chicken and sauce from the plastic bag to the garlic and olive oil there. Close the lid and set 15 minutes of cooking time.

5. Serve sprinkled with the chopped cilantro. Serve with white Jasmine rice and vegetables.

Insta-Chicken

Prep Time: 5 minutes

Cook Time: 15 minutes

Servings: 4

Ingredients

1 lb. chicken breasts, boneless, skinless &frozen

1/2 cup water

1/2 cup flavorful liquid of choice

Directions

1. Combine water and preferred flavorful liquid in a small bowl. Place the chicken in the Instant Pot, and pour the liquid it.

2. Seal lid, press the Poultry button, adjust cooking time to 15 minutes for standard chicken breasts of 4-6 oz. each, and 30 minutes pressure cooking time for extra-large chicken breasts of1 lb. each.

3. When beep sounds, quick release and remove lid. Remove the chicken breasts to a platter and shred into pieces with forks.

4. If the sauce is too thin, set Instant Pot on 'Sauté' mode to reduce to your taste while still shredding the chicken. Place the shredded chicken back to the sauce and toss well to coat.

Romano Chicken
Ingredients:

1 tablespoon of all-purpose flour

1 onion minced

½ teaspoon salt

½ teaspoon pepper

6 boneless skinless chicken, cut into chunks

2 tbsp oil

1 (10-ounce) can tomato sauce

1 (4-ounce can) sliced mushrooms

1 teaspoon vinegar

1 tbsp sugar

1 tbsp dried oregano

1 teaspoon dried basil

1 teaspoon chicken bouillon granules

1 cup Romano cheese

1 teaspoon garlic – minced

1 tbsp butter, at room temperature

Directions

1. Sauté chicken in oil until brown. Add onion and garlic until translucent. Add the remaining ingredients except the flour, butter and Romano cheese and stir to combine.

2. Lock Instant Pot lid into place. Select the manual option and adjust to 10-minutes of cooking time.

3. When done, leave for 10-minutes then release pressure.

4. Remove lid, add the Romano cheese and stir. Thicken sauce by adding a mixture of butter and flour. Add this paste to the cooked sauce to thicken it.

5. Serve over rice or pasta or enjoy alone.

PORK RECIPES

Easy Green Chili
Ingredients:

1 pound of pork

1 cup green salsa

Directions:

1. Cut the pork into sizes of stew meat and cook on the Sauté/Browning mode until brown.

2. Pour the salsa over it and then cook on the Meat & Stew mode for 20 to 30 minutes.

3. Wait for 5 minutes, open the lid and quick release pressure. Serve and enjoy!

Pork Carnitas In Instant Pot

Servings: 6 – 8

Ingredients

3- 4 pound pork shoulder roast

2 tablespoons coconut oil

3 cloves garlic

1 tablespoon ground ancho chili powder

2 teaspoons ground cumin

Juice of 2 oranges

2 teaspoons ground chipotle chili powder

1 teaspoon coriander

1 tablespoons salt

½ teaspoon oregano

1 bottle of lager beer

2 bay leaves

1 onion, quartered

Directions

1. In a small bowl, combine the chipotle chili powder, ancho chili powder, oregano, coriander, cumin and salt. Cut the pork into 2 inch cubes and rub the spice mixture all over.

2. Press the Sauté option on your Instant Pot and melt the coconut oil. Brown on all sides in batches, remove and set aside.

3. Add the orange juice and beer to the pot, scraping up any browned bit from the bottom of the pot. Now add the garlic, onion and bay leaves and

place the browned pork pieces on top. Cover, lock lid and select the Meat/Stew button.

4. When cooked, remove roast from pot but leave the cooking liquid. Press sauté again and simmer the cooking liquid until it has been reduced by half.

5. Set your broiler oven on high temperature. While the liquid is simmering, shred the meat and place on a sheet pan.

6. When the liquid has been reduced by half, turn off pot, spoon some of the cooking liquid over the pork. Broil the pork meat until crisp and brown.

7. Serve with guacamole, salsa, lime wedges and hot tortillas.

Pork Hock With Agaricus Mushrooms

This is a very scrumptious pork dish that even tastes better with rice.

Prep Time: 20 minutes

Cook Time: 40-45 minutes

Stand Time: 4 hours

Servings: 6

Ingredients

20 dry agaricus mushrooms

2 lb boneless pork hock, cut into 1-inch cubes

1 anise star

1 green onion, chopped to 2-inch long

1 tablespoon olive oil

1 tsp fresh ginger, sliced

2 cloves

1 tablespoon cooking wine

1 teaspoon dark vinegar

1 tablespoon light soy sauce

1 teaspoon sugar

1 tablespoon dark soy sauce

1/2 teaspoon salt

Directions:

1. Soak the agaricus mushrooms in lots of cold water for 4-5 hours, rinse and set aside.

2. Place the pork inside the Instant Pot and fill it with boiling water, press the "Sauté" button then the "Adjust" button to set the temperature to "More". Boil 2 minutes and then rinse under cold water.

3. Clean the inner pot and dry with a paper towel. Press the "Sauté" button then the "Adjust" button to set temperature to "More". Add olive oil and sauté green onion, anise cloves and ginger for 1 minute.

4. Now add cooking wine and sauté 30 seconds. Return the pork hock meat to the Pot, and sauté 1 or 2 minutes. Add the soaked agaricus mushrooms, mixing thoroughly.

5. Add dark vinegar, sugar, light soy sauce and dark soy sauce, mixing well. Secure lid and place the pressure valve to the "Seal" position. Set button to "Manual" and 35 minutes cooking time.

6. Once done, wait for 5 more minutes. Release the pressure slowly then open the lid. Select "Sauté", set temperature to "More" and stir until the sauce reduces to 1/3.

7. Remove the cooked meat to a serving dish and serve over rice.

Steamed Ribs In Black Soy Bean Sauce And Garlic

Prep Time: 15 minutes

Cook Time: 6 minutes

Servings: 6

Ingredients

1lb Pork ribs

1 tablespoon olive oil

1½tablespoons freshly minced garlic

1 tablespoon of minced Chinese salted & fermented soy beans (black)

1 small fresh chili pepper, finely chopped

1 teaspoon green onion for garnish, freshly chopped

Marinade Ingredients:

½ tablespoon of dark soy sauce

1½ tablespoons of Kikkoman light soy sauce

1 teaspoon sugar

1/3 teaspoon salt

2 tablespoons water

1½ tablespoons corn starch

Directions

1. Clean the ribs and cut between bones into pieces. Add ribs and the marinade ingredients to a Ziploc bag, seal and mix thoroughly. Refrigerate overnight.

2. Add olive oil to sauté pan and sauté garlic, Chinese salted fermented soy beans and chili pepper on medium heat for 30 seconds. Mix with the marinated ribs in a bowl.

3. Place steam rack inside your Instant Pot and add water to the 2-cup level. Put the bowl on the steam rack. Seal lid, press the "Steam" button and cook 6 minutes.

4. When done, wait 5 minutes. Release the pressure slowly then open the lid. Remove steamed ribs and garnish with 1 teaspoon of chopped green onions.

Braised Ribs With Spirulina And Woodears

Get your dried spirulina and woodears from the Chinese grocery store nearest to you and prepare this awesomely tasty dinner dish.

Prep Time: 15 minutes

Cook Time: 30 minutes

Servings: 6

Ingredients:

1½ lb baby back ribs, membranes removed

5 small dried Chinese mushrooms

¼ oz dried black Chinese fungus (black woodears)

½ oz dried spirulina

1½ tbsp olive oil

2 green onions washed and chopped to 1 inch long

2-3 slices of ginger

1 anise star

2 cloves

1 tbsp cooking wine

3/4 tsp salt

1 ½ tsp sugar

1½ tbsp light soy sauce

1½ tbsp premium soy sauce

1½ tbsp dark soy sauce

Directions:

1. Soak the dried mushrooms and the black fungus in cold water for 2-4hours, rinse and drain. Soak dried spirulina in cold water for 1 hour, rinse and drain and then set aside. Wash ribs, cut into pieces, rinse and drain.

2: Heat olive oil in a sauté pan over high temperature, sauté sliced ginger, chopped green onion, cloves and anise star for 30 seconds.

3. Add pork ribs, stir and cook for 3-4 minutes until slightly brown outside. Add cooking wine and then remove from heat.

4. Place ribs inside the Instant Pot, add the premium soy sauce, dark soy sauce, light soy sauce, salt, sugar, black fungus and mushrooms. Cover lid and place the pressure valve to "Seal". Cook 18 minutes.

5. Once done, release pressure, open the lid and add the spirulina. Cover the lid, place pressure valve to "Seal" and cook 2 minutes.

6. When the program is done, release the pressure and open the lid. Remove to a serving bowl and serve with steamed rice.

Classic Cassoulet

With your Instant pot, you get to cook this classic provincial French dish in just an hour!

Servings: 4-6

Ingredients:

2 pounds boneless pork ribs, cut into 1-inch chunks

1 cup beef broth

4 cloves garlic, minced

2 cups great northern beans

2 tablespoons olive oil

2 cups herbed croutons

1 carrot, diced

1 celery stalk, diced

½ white onion, diced

2 tablespoons dried rosemary

Salt and pepper to taste

1 cup goat cheese, crumbled, optional

Directions

1. In a large skillet, heat olive oil to medium high heat. Sprinkle the pork ribs with salt and pepper, then brown on all sides in the skillet.

2. Place the pork in the Instant Pot; add the beans, carrot, broth, celery, rosemary, onion and garlic. Lock lid into place and cook 35 minutes on the stew setting. Ladle into large soup bowls, top with croutons and goat cheese.

Braised Pork Ribs In Soy Sauce

Prep Time: 5 minutes

Cook Time: 45 minutes

Servings: 6

Ingredients:

2 lb spareribs

1 tbsp olive oil

3-4 fresh ginger, sliced

1 green onion, rinsed & cut into 2 inches length

1 star anise

2 cloves

11/2 tbsp anka sauce or 11/2 tsp red yeast rice

1 tbsp cooking wine

11/2 tablespoons premium dark soy sauce

1 tablespoon light soy sauce

1 tablespoon premium light soy sauce

1/2 tsp salt

1 1/2 tablespoons honey

4 tbsp water

Directions:

1. Wash ribs with warm water and cut into small pieces. Soak 2 minutes in boiling water. Drain, rinse and drain again.

2, Add oil to Instant Pot, select the "Sauté" option and add ginger, green onion, cloves and anise and sauté 1 minute on high. Add red yeast rice or anka sauce and ribs, stir and cook 2 minutes.

3. Add cooking wine and stir occasionally. Add cooking wine, premium dark soy sauce, light soy sauce, salt, honey and water. Cover lid and place pressure valve to "Seal". Set on "Manual" mode and cook 35 minutes.

4. When done, wait 5 minutes. Release the pressure slowly then open the lid. Select "Sauté" and set on "high", stir a few time until the sauce reduces to 1/4.

5. Place the cooked pork into to a bowl and serve over rice.

Sweet & Tasty Cranberry Pulled Pork

Out of cranberry season? Use frozen cranberries for this yummy recipe. Alternatively, you can use other kind of fruits such as plums, blueberries or cherries. Any of them will be fantastic!

Prep Time: 10 minutes

Cook Time: 85 minutes

Servings: 6

Ingredients

1 tablespoon fat of choice

2 tablespoons chopped fresh herbs (marjoram, oregano and/or sage)

2 lbs boneless pork roast

12 oz cranberries

10 oz bone broth

2 tablespoons apple cider vinegar

1 tablespoon honey

1/8 tsp ground cloves

¼ tsp cinnamon

¼ teaspoon of granulated garlic

Sea salt

Directions

1. Set Instant Pot to sauté. Pour fat into the bottom of pot and use a spatula to spread around.

2. Salt pork liberally on all sides, place in hot oil and sear for 2 minutes per side (uncovered) until lightly browned.

3. Set Instant Pot to the manual setting for 70 minutes. Add broth and cranberries to the bottom of the pot and then sprinkle herbs, apple cider vinegar and honey on top. Close lid and cook 70 minutes.

4. Release pressure using the release valve, transfer pork to a cutting board and shred with two forks.

5. Place back in the Pot, sprinkle with sea salt, and set for 10 more minutes to allow the pork absorb the broth, and make it more flavorful and juicy.

6. Remove the cranberries and pork from the liquid to a platter. Toss with the garlic, cloves and cinnamon and serve warm.

Pressure Cooker Kakuni

Have a taste of Japan by trying this great-tasting Japanese recipe.

Prep Time: 5 minutes

Cook Time: 45 minutes

Total Time: 50 minutes

Servings: 3-4

Ingredients

2 lb. pork belly block

3 green onions

1 tablespoon of vegetable oil

½ cup water

4 boiled eggs

½ cup soy sauce

¼ cup sake

½ cup mirin

1 inch ginger

¼ cup sugar

Japanese 7 spices (Shichimi Togarashi) for taste, optional

Water

Seasonings

Directions

1. Cut the green part of the onions in half. Peel and slice ginger thinly. Press the "Sauté" function on your Instant Pot and heat the oil and then cook the pork belly.

2. Pour water to cover the pork, add the green onions and ginger and secure lid. The steam release handle should point at "sealing" and not "venting". Select the Keep "Warm/Cancel" button to stop cooking.

3. Press the "meat/Stew" button and cook 35 minutes under pressure. Once done, let the pressure release naturally or slide to the "Venting" position to release steam. Open lid, drain the water and discard the ginger and green onion. Rinse the pork belly with warm water.

4. Return the meat to the Instant Pot; add sake, mirin, ½ cup water, sugar and soy sauce. Mix the seasonings and add the boiled eggs. Select the "Sauté" button and press "Adjust" to increase the heat. Simmer to let the alcohol evaporate.

4. Once it evaporates, select the "Keep Warm/Cancel" button to turn the Sauté mode off. Secure lid. Press the "meat/Stew" button to cook and set time to 10 minutes.

5. Once done, press the "Sauté" button, simmer on low heat until the liquid has reduced by half.

6. Serve the pork belly, boiled egg and green vegetables, if any, over rice. To make it spicier, sprinkle Japanese 7 spices (shichimi toagarashi) over it.

Braised Pork Hock &Potatoes

This very tasty dish goes really well with or noodles or rice.

Prep Time: 20 minutes

Cook Time: 40-45 minutes

Servings: 6

Ingredients

2 lb boneless pork hock, cut into cubes of1-inch &rinsed under cold water

7 small potatoes, peeled & rinsed

1 tbsp olive oil

1 green onion, cut into 2-inch long

1tbsp fresh ginger, sliced

1 anise star

2 cloves

1 tbsp cooking wine

1 tsp dark vinegar

11/2 tsp sugar

2 tbsp light soy sauce

1 tbsp dark soy sauce

1tbsp light soy sauce

1/3 tsp salt

1 tbsp olive oil

Directions:

1. Place diced pork inside the Instant Pot, and fill with boiling water. Press Sauté button then press Adjust to set temperature to "More". Boil 3-5 minutes and then rinse under cold water.

2. Clean the inner pot and dry it. Select Sauté, set temperature to "More". Add 1 tablespoon of olive oil and sauté green onion, ginger, anise star, cloves for 1 minute.

3. Add cooking wine and sauté another minute. Return cooked meat back to the Instant Pot, and sauté for 1 or 2 minutes.

4. Add dark vinegar, sugar, light soy sauce, dark soy sauce, 1tbsp light soy sauce and 1/3 tsp salt, mixing well. Lock lid, set pressure valve to the Seal position. Press the manual button and set timer for 35 minutes.

5. Meanwhile, cut the potatoes into 4 equal parts, rinse and then pat dry. Place a non-stick pan on high heat, add 1 tbsp of olive oil and cook potato pieces until golden brown.

6. When the Instant Pot beeps, wait 5 more minutes and slowly release the pressure. Open the lid and transfer meat to a bowl, cover to keep warm.

7. Press the Sauté button on Normal temperature and cook the potato pieces with the meat sauce for 7 to 8 minutes

8. Place cooked meat in the pressure cooker and stir gently 1 minute. Remove to a platter and serve with rice.

Braised Pork Ribs With Bamboo Shoots And Garlic

This great- tasting dish goes well with steamed rice.

Prep Time: 10 minutes

Stand Time: 8 hours

Cook Time: 45 minutes

Servings: 6

Ingredients:

2lb spare ribs, membrane removed

¼ cup winter shoots, dried

1 tablespoon of olive oil

2-3 fresh ginger, sliced

2 green onion rinsed & cut into 2-inch length

5-6 garlic cloves

1 star anise

1 tablespoon cooking wine

2 tablespoon premium dark soy sauce

11/2 tbsp light soy sauce

1/2 tsp salt

3 tbsp water

½ teaspoon of sugar

1 teaspoon of sesame oil

Directions:

1. Soak the dried bamboo shoots in cold water for 8 straight hours. Rinse and drain. Wash ribs and cut them into small pieces between bones; rinse and drain.

2. Heat olive oil in a non-stick pan over high heat. Sauté green onion, star anise, ginger and garlic for 1-2 minutes. Add the pork ribs; cook for 3to 4 minutes or until the ribs start turning brown.

3. Add bamboo shoots, sautéing for 1-2 more minutes. Now add coking wine, premium dark soy sauce, light soy sauce, salt, sugar and water and bring to a boil.

4. Place all the contents into an Instant Pot pressure cooker, cover, "Seal" the pressure valve, select "Manual" function and set timer for 36 minutes.

5. When done, wait 5 minutes, release the pressure slowly and open the lid. Press "Sauté" and set the temperature to "More", stir every now and then until the sauce is reduced to a quarter.

6. Transfer to a bowl. Serve over rice and enjoy.

Simple Pork Chops

For your perfect, juicy pork chops, try this recipe.

Ingredients:

3-4 Pork Chops, ½ - ¾ inch thick

1 egg, beaten

½ cup onions, chopped

2- 4 garlic cloves, squashed &chopped

Flour

1 tbsp butter

Salt and pepper

Bread crumbs

1-2 tbsp vegetable oil

2 -3tablespoons water

Directions

1. Set Instant Pot on sauté and heat the oil and butter until hot. Dredge pork chops in flour, bread crumbs and dip into beaten egg.

2. Brown pork chops on both sides. Remove and put on a plate. Add in the onions, stir for about a minute then add the garlic and stir.

3. Set to steam mode and add water. Put the steamer in pot and place browned pork chops on the steamer above the water and drippings. Lock lid into place. Steam 5 minutes and remove.

4. Pour dripping over pork chops or make gravy with a little flour and water.

Pork Chops Cheese Soup With Arborio Rice
Ingredients:

1/2 cup Arborio rice

2 tablespoons of oil

2 pork chops, center cut

1 can cheddar cheese soup

1/2 cup chopped onion

1/2 cup corn (kernels cut off one ear)

1/4 fresh tomato, chopped

Salt/pepper to taste

1¾ cup water

Directions:

1. Sauté onion and pork chops in oil until light brown. Now add the other ingredients and stir thoroughly.

2. Cover Instant Pot and cook for 8 minutes.

3. Wait for 1-2 minutes to bring pressure down. Remove lid, stir well. Add some Parmesan and serve.

Pressure Cooker Kalua Pork

Enjoy this simplified and delicious version of the traditional Hawaiian Kālua Pork recipe.

Prep Time: 5 minutes

Cook Time: 110 minutes

Servings: 4

Ingredients:

4 lb Pork shoulder, roast, cut in two pieces

1 tbsp Hickory liquid smoke (Wright's)

1/2 cup water

2 teaspoon of Kosher or Hawaiian salt

Directions:

1. Pre-heat cooker by pressing sauté and add oil when hot. Brown roasts in 2 batches and transfer to a plate when browned.

2. Turn off pressure cooker and add water and liquid smoke to it. Add the browned roasts and any accumulated juices as well. Sprinkle salt over the pork roasts.

3. Select the manual button and set 90 minutes of cooking time. When the program is completed, release pressure naturally and carefully remove lid.

4. Remove the meat, shred and discard excess fat. Add juices from the Instant pot to moisten the meat.

Green Lentil Cassoulet With Pancetta And Chicken
To peel garlic cloves quickly, immerse in boiling water for 3-5 seconds.

Servings: 8

Ingredients:

2, 1/2-inch-thick slices of pancetta (4 oz), cut into 1/2-inch dice

1 lemon-pepper rotisserie chicken, skin discarded& cut into pieces

5 tablespoons of extra-virgin olive oil

1 pound French green lentils

1 medium onion, cut into 1/2-inch dice

4 fresh thyme sprigs

1 quart chicken broth

1 large garlic, separated into cloves &peeled

3/4 pound garlic salami, sliced diagonally 1/2 inch thick

4 ounces lean slab bacon, cut into 1-inch cubes

4 tablespoons parsley, chopped

2 quarts water

Kosher salt to taste

Directions

1. Use the Sauté option to heat 3 tablespoons of olive oil. Add the onion and pancetta and cook about 5 minutes or until the fat has been rendered. Add the chicken broth, lentils, water, thyme, garlic, salami, bacon and chicken.

2. Seal lid. Set on Manual to cook 15 minutes. Wait 10 minutes. Release pressure and remove the lid.

3. Discard thyme. Add salt to taste. Set on Sauté to thicken the sauce. Add parsley, stir and serve.

BEEF RECIPES

One Pot Beef Roast With Potatoes & Carrots
Servings: 6-8

Ingredients

2lbs potatoes, roughly cubed

2-4lb beef roast

1 1/2 cup stock

1 tablespoons of olive oil

1 bunch of parsley, chopped

1lb thick carrots, peeled

1 cup red wine

61

2 tablespoon fresh thyme

4 tablespoon unsalted butter

4 tablespoon pistachio, chopped

Directions

1. Preheat cooker by pressing the Sauté button. Add olive oil and sear roast on all sides. De-glaze the pot with chicken stock.

2. Seal lid, press manual button and set 45-50 minutes of cooking time. Open and quick release pressure. Add the potatoes and carrots.

3. Seal lid, press Manual and select 10 minutes pressure cooking time. When program ends, open and quick release pressure.

4. Remove carrots to a platter and slice. Remove the potatoes and place on the platter. Remove roast, and place on aluminum- foil tented plate and set aside.

5. Pass cooking liquid through a strainer and return to the Instant Pot. Add butter and wine and press sauté to reduce the liquid in the cooker. Uncover pot.

6. Slice roast, serve with potatoes and carrots. Pour a little of the reduced cooking liquid over it and sprinkle with nuts and thyme.

Sweet And Sour Spareribs

Prep Time: 10 minutes

Cook Time: 15 minutes

Servings: 4-6

Ingredients

4 lbs ribs, trimmed& cut

1 tablespoon oil

1/4 cup ketchup

1 medium onion sliced

1/4 soy sauce

1/3 cup rice wine (or cider) vinegar

1/3 cup brown sugar

1 20 oz can pineapple

2 cloves garlic, chopped

1 teaspoon ginger, finely chopped

1 teaspoon chili powder

1 teaspoon ground coriander

1 teaspoon fish sauce (optional)

Pinch of smoked paprika

Corn starch slurry

Salt and pepper to taste

Directions

1. Add oil to your Instant Pot 6-in-1 Pressure Cooker and sauté onions until translucent.

2. Add all the ingredients except the cornstarch slurry. (Spareribs must be submerged in sauce).

3. Pressure cook 12 minutes on "Stew", switch to keep- warm for 3 minutes. Release pressure. Check the meat for moisture and doneness. If more time is needed, set timer to "Stew" for 2-4 more minutes.

4. Once meat is done, transfer to bowl, taste for seasoning and adjust accordingly. Set to sauté, once the sauce starts to boil, thicken as desired with cornstarch slurry, stirring 1 minute.

5. Serve with rice and vegetables of your choice.

Cabernet Short Ribs With Watercress Fettuccine Alfredo
Servings: 4

Ingredients:

8 beef short ribs

1 package fettuccine

1 cup beef broth

2 tablespoons canola oil

1 cup cabernet sauvignon

½ bulb fennel, sliced

1 tablespoon stone ground mustard

1 tablespoon red wine vinegar

4 cloves garlic, crushed

2 tablespoons olive oil

½ cup butter

2 bunches watercress, trimmed

1 pint heavy whipping cream

2 cups asiago cheese, grated

1 tablespoon rosemary, finely chopped

1 teaspoon nutmeg

Salt and pepper to taste

Directions:

1. Season beef short ribs with salt and pepper. In a large skillet, heat the canola oil to medium-high heat and add the beef short ribs. Sear 2-3 minutes per side.

2. Place beef short ribs in the Instant Pot and add the beef broth, fennel and cabernet sauvignon. Seal lid, select the beef setting and cook 35 minutes.

3. Meanwhile, whisk together the olive oil, mustard, red wine vinegar and garlic in a medium bowl. Add the watercress and set aside.

4. Melt the butter in a medium saucepan on low-medium heat. Whisk in the heavy whipping cream. Add the asiago cheese a little at a time and melt completely. Add the nutmeg and rosemary, stirring to blend. Keep this sauce on low heat until ready to use.

5. At the last15 minutes of cooking the beef ribs, bring a large pot of salted water to a boil. Add the fettuccine and cook as instructed. Strain, add to the saucepan containing the sauce and stir well.

6. Divide onto plates and top with dressed watercress. Take out the ribs from the Instant Pot and place 2 ribs on top the watercress on each plate. Enjoy!

Pressure Cooked Beef Stew

Prep Time: 15 minutes

Cook Time: 35 minutes

Servings: 6

Ingredients

6 medium sized red potatoes halved

3 lbs. beef chuck roast, cut into in. pieces

2 red bell peppers cut into 2 in. pieces

1 large onion quartered

5 large carrots halved

3 stocks celery cut into 1 inch pieces

8 cloves fresh garlic chopped coarsely

1 cup beef stock

1 cup vegetable stock

1/2 – 6oz. can tomato paste

1 – 8oz. can tomato sauce

2 tablespoon corn starch or flower diluted

2 tablespoon Worcestershire sauce

1 teaspoon garlic powder

1 teaspoon onion powder

1 teaspoon dried thyme

3 bay leaves

1 & 1/2 teaspoon of fresh ground salt

1 & 1/2 teaspoon fresh ground pepper

1/2 cup water

2 tablespoon of virgin olive oil

Directions

1. Season the meat with salt and pepper. Press sauté on the pressure cooker to brown in olive oil.

2. Deglaze with some beef broth. (Brown half of the meat at a time.) Add garlic to the browned meat and sauté another minute. Turn pressure cooker off.

3. Add the rest of the ingredients with carrots and potatoes last. Secure lid. Set timer to cook for 35 minutes on high pressure.

4. Release pressure naturally for 10 minutes and then quick release remaining pressure. Serve and enjoy!

Mexican styled Lamb BBQ

By using the meat setting on your Instant Pot, you get to save some slow cooking time. That way, you get to enjoy this southern Mexican-styled lamb dish with friends and family.

Servings: 3-4

Ingredients:

3 lb lamb shoulder

1 19-oz can Enchilada sauce (I use Old El Paso)

1 Spanish onion

2 tablespoons of oil

3 garlic cloves, minced

Salt to taste

For Servings:

Cilantro, chopped without the stems

Black beans or refried beans

12-16 corn tortillas

Limes, cut into 8ths

Chipotle style rice

Directions

1. Marinate the lamb overnight in the Enchilada sauce. Set Instant Pot on sauté, add oil and let it heat up 1-2 minutes. Add the onions and cook until soft then add garlic about 1 minute. Add the lamb and marinade and then heat up.

2. Set Instant Pot on stew setting and cook for 45 minutes on natural pressure release.

3. Meanwhile, heat the beans, cut limes and pour the hot rice into a bowl.

4. Shred cooked lamb with two forks and transfer to a serving bowl. Spoon a lot of sauce over it. Heat up the corn tortillas.

5. Serve by spooning rice and beans onto the soft, warm corn tortilla, sprinkle cilantro on it, add lamb, and squeeze some lime juice all over. Alternatively, spoon lamb mixture onto the corn tortilla, sprinkle on cilantro and then squeeze on lime juice.

Red Wine Sauce Beef Grilling Ribs

Prep Time: 15 minutes

Cook Time: 90 minutes

Servings: 6

Ingredients

3½ lb beef grilling ribs

1/2 cup all-purpose flour

½ teaspoon black pepper

2 teaspoons salt

3 tablespoons olive oil

1 purple onion, peeled and sliced

3-4 cloves garlic crushed

1 small ripe tomato, chopped

3 tablespoons ketchup

Half bottle (400ml) red wine

½ teaspoon dry thyme

1 teaspoon of dry parsley

½ teaspoon dry rosemary

11/2 teaspoons salt

1 teaspoon sugar

½ cup of water

Directions

1. Add flour, salt and black pepper to a Ziploc bag and mix thoroughly. Add the beef ribs to coat with flour mixture evenly. Shake excess flour off.

2. Add olive oil to a deep sauté pan, brown beef ribs on medium-high heat. Remove beef ribs to an Instant Pot.

3. In the same sauté pan, add onion and garlic and cook until onion becomes transparent. Add tomato and ketchup and sauté 1 minute. Add red wine, thyme, dry parsley, rosemary, salt, sugar and water and mix well.

4. Put cooked onions and sauce into the Instant Pot. Cover and seal the lid. Set cooking to manual and 60 minutes of cooking time.

5. When done, wait 15 minutes. Release the pressure slowly then open the lid. Transfer beef ribs to a serving bowl.

6. Pour the braising liquid into the sauté pan and remove excess fat on the surface with a spoon. Set heat at medium-high to reduce the sauce to about half its volume. Ladle sauce onto the beef ribs and serve.

Beef Bourguignon

Generally a Beef Bourguignon is complicated to prepare, it comprised of about several steps and takes all day. However, with your pressure cooker, you can make this lovely recipe in a couple of hours. It seems almost magical!

Servings: 3-4

Ingredients:

1 1/2 lbs lean beef chuck roast, boneless & cut into chunks

5 medium carrots cut into chunks

12 pearl onions, peeled

2/3 cup dry red wine

2 tablespoons tomato paste

8 oz mushrooms quarters

2 garlic cloves, minced

1 bay leaf

2 tablespoons fresh thyme

2/3 cup beef stock

1/4 teaspoon black pepper

2 tablespoons whole wheat flour

3/4 teaspoon salt

1/4 cup water

Directions

1. Dry beef and sauté in batches to brown on all sides and then set aside. Brown the pearl onions.

2. Add all ingredients, except the flour and water, cook on high for 12 minutes and natural release.

3. Once beep sounds, mix water and flour and pour into the pot. Cook until thickened or for 1minute.

Easy& Spicy Steak Dinner
Servings: 3-4

Ingredients:

1.5 lbs round Steak or flank steak, cut into small strips

3 crushed cloves or 3/4 teaspoon granulated garlic

1 – 8 oz Tomato Sauce

2 small green bell peppers

1 medium onion

2 tablespoons olive oil

2 tablespoons apple cider vinegar or white vinegar

3 roma tomatoes, diced

2 jalapeño peppers, diced

1 bunch fresh cilantro

1 cup of water

2 – 3 tablespoons general purpose flour

Directions:

1. Add all ingredients, except the flour, to the Instant Pot and mix well. Close lid, press the Meat/Stew button and set time to 25 minutes. When done, quick release and open lid carefully.

2. Pour 11/2 cup of the liquid in a bowl. Whisk in the flour gradually until a pasty texture is achieved.

3. Add the flour mixture to the stew and mix thoroughly. Serve over white rice.

Mediterranean Lamb Tagine
Servings: 4-6

Ingredients

21/2 -3 lbs lamb shoulder, cut into pieces

31/2 oz almonds, shelled, peeled &toasted

1 teaspoon cinnamon powder

1 teaspoon turmeric powder

1 teaspoon ginger powder

1 teaspoon cumin powder

2 onions, roughly sliced

3 tablespoons of honey

2 garlic cloves, crushed

10 oz prunes, soaked (or a mix of dry apricots and raisins)

1 cup vegetable stock

1 bay leaf

1 cinnamon stick

Salt & pepper to taste

Olive oil

Sesame seeds

Directions

1. Combine the turmeric, ground cinnamon, garlic ginger and 2 tbsp olive oil to make a paste. Cover meat with this paste and then set aside.

2. Cover the dried prunes in a bowl of boiling water and set aside. Pre-heat the cooker by pressing the sauté button. When hot, add two teaspoon of olive oil and onions and cook about 3 minutes or until softened

3. Remove the onions, and set aside. Add the meat, and brown about 10 minutes on all sides. De-glaze cooker with the vegetable stock. Add the onions, cinnamon stick and bay leaf.

4. Lock the lid, press Manual and choose 35 minutes cooking time. Naturally release pressure. Press sauté and add the honey and the rinsed and drained prunes.

5. Press sauté to reduce the liquid and to simmer. Remove cinnamon stick and the bay leaf. Sprinkle with sesame seeds and toasted almonds and serve.

Tasty Lamb Dinner

Servings: 4

Ingredients:

4 veal or lamb shanks, cut

¼ cup flour

2 medium carrots, chopped in large chunks

2 lbs red potatoes

¼ cup olive oil

2 stalks celery, cut into large chunks

½ tsp garlic powder

2 tbsp butter

1 tsp thyme

½ teaspoon onion powder

1 tbsp butter

1 teaspoon of rosemary

2 cloves crushed garlic

1 medium or large onion, chopped

1 to 2 cups chicken broth

½ tsp black pepper

½ tsp salt

Directions

1. Combine the flour and the seasonings in a large bowl. Blend together with a wire whisk. Rinse the shanks and dry. Roll each shank in the flour mix and place on a plate, set aside but keep the remaining flour.

2. Heat the oil to the pressure cooker and brown the shanks on all sides. Remove to a plate. Add the flour to the rest of the oil and make rue and then add the broth to loosen this rue into a sauce.

3. Next, pour half of the sauce in the Instant Pot and place each shank upright into the sauce. Add the veggies to fill the gaps. Pour the rest of the sauce over the veggies and shanks. Cover and cook for 90 minutes.

4. Few minutes before the cooking cycle ends, boil the red potatoes with the skin on until tender. Mash and add 2 tablespoons of butter. Season with salt and pepper.

5. Serve lamb shank with potatoes and vegetables and ladle with sauce from the Instant pot.

Corned Beef And Cabbage In The Instant Pot

Prep Time: 10 minutes

Cook Time: 105 minutes

Total Time: 1 hour 55 minutes

Servings: 8

Ingredients

3 cups beef broth

3-4 pound corned beef brisket

1 shallot or ¼ medium onion, peeled & roughly chopped

3 garlic cloves, peeled& whole

15 whole black peppercorns

3 bay leaves

9 allspice

5 sprigs fresh thyme

6 small to medium Red Potatoes, rinsed & cut into eighths, optional

5 carrots, peeled & cut into 2-3 inch pieces

2 shallots or ½ onion, minced

2 cloves garlic, minced

½ teaspoon kosher salt

1 head green cabbage, cut into 8 wedges

3 cups water

Directions

1. In the Instant Pot, place corned beef brisket with the fat side up. Add water, beef broth, shallot, garlic cloves, allspice, peppercorns, thyme and bay leaves.

2. Secure lid, place vent to "sealing". Press the Manual button, set cooking time to 90 minutes at High Pressure.

3. When cooking is completed, open the lid and let the pressure release naturally. Remove the corned beef from pot, reserving liquid for carrots, cabbage and potatoes, if using.

4. Cover the corned beef with foil and set aside. Use a slotted spoon to strain cooking liquid to remove fat, thyme and bay leaves. Place carrots, shallots, garlic, salt and optional potatoes into cooking liquid and then place cabbage on top.

5. Lock lid into place, place vent to "sealing". Press the Manual button, set cooking time to 15minutes at High Pressure. When cooking is completed, wait few seconds, open the lid and let the pressure release naturally.

6. Remove vegetables and serve with sliced corned beef.

Flavorful Braised Beef Shank In Soybean Paste

It's dinner time. Enjoy this flavorful and tender braised beef shank in soybean paste.

Prep Time: 10 minutes

Cook Time: 45 minutes

Stand Time: 30 minutes

Servings: 8

Ingredients

2lb beef shank

2 tablespoons olive oil

1 tablespoon chili bean paste

1 tablespoon sweet soybean paste

2 green onions, cut to 2-inch length

2 teaspoons fresh ginger, sliced

5-6 garlic cloves, crushed

1 teaspoon Chinese cooking wine

1 tablespoon light soy sauce

1 tablespoon dark soy sauce

2 teaspoons sugar

1/3 teaspoon salt

3-4 tablespoons water

Directions:

1. Soak beef 30 minutes in cold water, drain and dice.

2. Place a pan on high heat and add 1 tablespoon of olive oil and beef. Sauté 3-5 minutes until beef turns brown and water evaporates. Remove beef to a bowl and set aside.

3. Heat 1 tablespoon of olive oil over medium-high heat in the same pan. Sauté chili bean paste and sweet soybean paste 30-40 seconds.

4. Add ginger, green onion and garlic; keep sautéing for 30 seconds. Return beef back to pan and sauté 1 minute. Add the Chinese cooking wine, light soy sauce, dark soy sauce, sugar, salt and water.

5. Transfer beef and sauce to the Instant Pot. Lock lid into place and position the pressure valve to "Seal". Press the "Manual" button and cook 38 minutes.

6. When the beep sounds, wait 5 minutes and release the pressure slowly and then open the lid. Press "Sauté", set temperature to "More" and stir infrequently until the sauce reduces to 1/3.

7. Transfer to a serving bowl and serve over rice.

Honey &Thyme Red Wine Pot Roast

Servings: 6-8

Ingredients

2 pounds russet potatoes, peeled & cut into 1½- 2-inch cubes

1 bottom round roast, about 4 lbs.

5 tablespoons vegetable oil

3 small onions, medium diced

1 head garlic (about 10 -12 cloves), lightly smashed

2 cups low-sodium chicken, beef, or vegetable broth

1 pound carrots (about 4 medium), roughly cut into pieces of 1 1/2-inch

2 cups medium-bodied red wine

5 to 6 sprigs fresh thyme

2 1/2 tablespoons honey

Salt and freshly ground black pepper

Directions

1. Add all ingredients, except the potatoes and carrots, to the Instant Pot, select the manual function and cook for 45 minutes at high pressure.

2. Quick release pressure; add carrots and potatoes and cook for 10 more minutes, release pressure naturally.

Lamb Rack Casserole

Servings: 6-8

Ingredients

1 pound of baby potatoes

1 pound rack of lamb

2 medium size tomatoes

2 teaspoon of Paprika

2 carrots

2 stalks of celery

1 large onion

3-4 large cloves of garlic

2 cups of chicken stock

3 table spoons of sherry or red wine

2 teaspoon of cumin powder

2 tablespoons of ketchup

A pinch of dried oregano leaves

A pinch of dried rosemary

A splash of beer

1-2 teaspoons of salt

Directions

1. Wash all vegetables; cut carrots and potatoes into 1 inch cubes. Dice the onion, garlic and tomatoes. Divide the rack of lamb into two.

2. Add all the ingredients to your instant pot, close lid, press the Stew/Meat button, and adjust time to 35 minutes cooking time.

3. When the program is completed, wait a few minutes to allow the Instant Pot cool down, release the pressure by turning the handle to the "Vent" position.

4. Open the lid and serve over multigrain rice.

Braised Beef Shank With Soy Sauce And Spices

A wonderful cold dish Chinese recipe you and your family will love.

Prep Time: 15 minutes

Cook Time: 35 minutes

Stand Time: 36 hours

Servings: 6

Ingredients

2lb Baby beef shank

Marinate Ingredients

2 teaspoon pepper cones, rinsed

1 teaspoon sugar

3 tablespoons Kikkoman light soy sauce

1 teaspoon salt

Sauce Ingredients

2 teaspoon salt

2 teaspoon sugar

1/2 cup Kikkoman light soy sauce

3 tablespoons dark soy sauce

3 garlic cloves

2 anises

11/2 teaspoon cumin

1tablespoon Jasmine green tea

2 bay leaves

2 teaspoons sesame oil

1 tsp fresh ginger, shredded

2 green onion, chopped

5cups water

Directions

1. in a Ziploc bag, put the baby beef shank and all the marinate ingredients, seal, shake well and refrigerate for a day.

2. Place beef shank in the Instant Pot, add all the sauce ingredients. Cover and seal lid. Press the "Manual" function and set time to 35 minutes.

3. When done, wait 10 minutes, release pressure slowly then open the lid. Remove the cooked beef shank to a clean bowl and refrigerate for 4 hours, slice and serve.

VEGETABLE RECIPES

Maple Beans & Bacon

Great beans in less than 1 hour, from start to finish!

Servings: 4

Ingredients:

3 cups navy or great northern beans

4 slices bacon or 1/2 cup bacon bits, cooked &chopped

5 cups chicken broth

2 heaping tablespoons sauce

1/2 onion, diced

2 tablespoons ketchup

Fancy molasses to taste

4 cups water

Salt and pepper to taste

Directions:

1. Measure out beans; wash rinse and cover with boiling water. Let it sit a few minutes.

2. Drain beans, and add to instant pot, together with all the ingredients. (Broth should cover beans by 1 inch but add more broth if necessary).

3. Season with salt and pepper. Set Instant Pot on beans mode.

4. Once cooked, serve and enjoy.

Eggplant And Pesto Stuffed Peppers
A mix of vegetables for your dinner relish.

Ingredients:

1pound ground beef

2 cups cooked rice

1medium onion, chopped

2 garlic cloves

1 eggplant

1 cup pesto

6 bell peppers

Olive oil

1 cup water

Salt and pepper to taste

Directions:

1. Slice the eggplant, season with enough salt and drain 30 minutes to reduce bitterness.

2. Pour a generous amount of olive oil in a pan and sauté the eggplant 5-10 minutes or until soft. Remove from pan.

3. Next, brown the ground beef, add garlic and onion, and cook until done. Add the cooked rice, eggplant pesto, and salt and pepper to taste.

3. Meanwhile, cut the tops off the green pepper, take out the seeds, chop up tops and add them to the ground beef mixture. Stuff the peppers with ground beef mixture.

4. Now add water to your Instant Pot, place trivet on the bottom, and stand the stuffed peppers upright in the pot.

5. Press the Manual function and set 3 minutes. Quick release and remove peppers. Serve topped with fresh chopped tomatoes and feta cheese.

Easy Caramelized Carrots

Delicious caramelized carrots for you to snack on.

Ingredients

1-2 tablespoons of butter

2 large carrots, peeled and cut

1/4 tsp baking soda

Directions

1. Melt the butter in your Instant Pot. Add the carrots and baking soda and stir.

2. Pressure cook 4-5 minutes

Black Eye Peas Delight

Simple and just perfect for you and your partner.

Ingredients:

1/2 lb bag black eyed peas, dried

1 tablespoon olive oil

3 ½ cups broth or water

1 ½ cups diced frozen onion

1 tablespoon oregano

1 1/2 teaspoons salt

Directions:

1. Add all to your instant pot

2. Press the bean/chili button and once cook, release steam naturally.

3. Serve and enjoy

Summer Boiled Peanut Salad
Ingredients

2 medium tomatoes, chopped

1 pound raw peanuts in shell, shelled

1/2 cup diced green pepper

1 bay leaf

2 tablespoons olive oil

1/2 cup sweet onion, diced

1/4 cup hot peppers, finely diced

1/4 cup celery, diced

2 tablespoons fresh lemon juice

3/4 teaspoon salt

1/4 teaspoon of freshly ground black pepper

2 cups water

Directions

1. Skin peanuts by blanching them in boiling salt water for a minute and then drain. Remove skins and discard.

2. Add peanuts to Instant Pot; add the 2 cups of water and bay leaf. Cook 20 minutes under pressure. Drain.

3. In a large bowl, add together peanuts and vegetables. Add the lemon juice, oil, salt and pepper, mixing well.

4. Pour over the salad mixture, tossing to combine.

Curry & Chickpea stuffed Acorn Squash

Prep Time: 25 minutes

Cook Time: 30 minutes

Total Time: 55 minutes

Servings: 2

Ingredients

¼ cup brown rice, washed & soaked for 30 min.

¾ cup dry chickpeas

1 small acorn squash, halved and deseeded

1 teaspoon oil

$\frac{1}{2}$ teaspoon of cumin seeds

$\frac{1}{2}$ cup red onion, chopped

4 garlic cloves, finely chopped

1 green chili, minced

$\frac{1}{2}$ inch ginger, minced

$\frac{1}{4}$ teaspoon turmeric

$\frac{1}{2}$ teaspoon garam masala

$\frac{1}{2}$ teaspoon dry mango powder (amchur) or $\frac{1}{2}$ tsp extra lime juice

$\frac{1}{2}$ teaspoon lime juice

2 small tomatoes, chopped

1 cup chopped greens, loosely packed (rainbow chard or spinach)

$\frac{1}{4}$ to $\frac{1}{2}$ teaspoon cayenne

$\frac{1}{2}$ teaspoon or more salt

2 cups water

Paprika, cilantro, and black pepper (for garnish)

Directions

1. Soak the chickpeas overnight but soak the brown rice for 30-40 minutes before preparation.

2. In an Instant Pot, add oil, press sauté and heat over medium sauté heat. Add cumin seeds and cook 1 minute until fragrant and change color.

3. Add onions, ginger, chili, garlic and a pinch of salt. Cook until translucent, about 5 minutes. Add spices, mix well and then add tomato, greens and lime juice, cook 4 to 5 minutes or until the tomatoes are saucy.

4. Add water to deglaze if needed. Add salt, chickpeas, cayenne, rice and 2 cups of water, mixing thoroughly.

5. To the pressure cooker, add one half or both halves of the squash, place squash in a steamer plate over the chickpea mixture. Secure lid and set cooking time to 15 or 20 minutes. Let the pressure release and open the lid.

6. Remove the steamer plate. Taste chickpea rice stew for salt and spice and adjust where necessary. Fill squash with chickpea rice mixture, garnish with black pepper and cilantro and serve.

Spinach& Lentil Night

Prep Time: 10 minutes

Cook Time: 20 minutes

Total Time: 30 minutes

Serving: 6

Ingredients

2 tablespoon of olive or coconut oil

1 large red or yellow onion, chopped

1 teaspoon ground turmeric

1 teaspoon ground cumin

3 cloves garlic, minced

1 teaspoon ground coriander

1/4 teaspoon dried cayenne pepper

1.5 cups of red lentils and/ or yellow split peas

1/2 teaspoon salt

1 large tomato, cut into 6-8 wedges

Handfuls (about 4 cups) of spinach

1/4 cup fresh cilantro, chopped (optional)

2 tsp butter (optional)

3 cups water

Directions

1. Add the olive or coconut oil to the pressure cooker, press 'sauté' and cook at medium sauté heat. Once the oil is hot, add the onions and cook until soften and translucent.

2. Add the garlic, cook 1 minute until fragrant. 'Cancel' to turn off heat. Add the coriander cumin, cayenne and turmeric, mixing well.

3. Add the lentils, tomato wedges, water and salt and then add to the onion mixture, stirring well. Cover pot with lid, and check that the valve is in a sealed position.

4. Next, press the 'Manual' button and set cooking time to 10 minutes. After 10 minutes, turn off warming mode by pressing 'Cancel', and wait for 10 minutes before opening valve to release pressure.

5. Remove and throw away tomato skins; whisk lentils to emulsify and smash the tomato wedges against the side of the pot. Add the spinach, cilantro and butter if using, stirring to mix. The residual heat will quickly wilt the spinach.

4. Serve with naan, brown rice, topped with fresh cilantro and plain yogurt.

Pressure-Steamed Artichokes

Prep Time: 5 minutes

Cook Time: 30 minutes

Servings: 2-4 as an appetizer

Ingredients

2 medium-sized whole artichokes (about 5 ½ ounces each)

1 cup water

1 lemon wedge

Directions

1. Rinse the artichokes and remove any outer leaves that are damaged. Trim off the stem and the top of the artichokes carefully. Rub the cut top with lemon to prevent browning.

2. Next, Set a steam rack into the Instant Pot's cooking, place the artichokes on top, and add water. Lock lid into place, select "Manual" function and adjust time to 20 minutes.

3. When program ends, press, "Cancel" to turn off the warming mode. Wait for 10 minutes, open the valve to release pressure. Remove the artichokes and serve warm with your preferred dipping sauce.

Red Lentils With Sweet Potato

Servings: 2

Ingredients:

1/2 cup red lentils, rinsed

1 sweet potato, peeled and chopped

1 small or medium onion, peeled & diced

1 tablespoon nutritional yeast flakes

1/2 tsp cinnamon

1/4 tsp garlic powder

1/4 tsp chipotle chili pepper powder

2 tablespoons of Sushi Rice Vinegar

1 1/2 cups water

Directions

1. Place all ingredients in the Instant Pot. Stir to combine.

2. Cook for 5 minutes on high pressure. Release the pressure.

3. Serve hot with over broccoli.

Butternut Squash & Ginger Soup

Servings: 4-6

Ingredients

4 lbs. butternut squash, peeled, seeded & cubed

1 large onion, chopped

1 sprig sage

2 cm (3/4") fresh ginger

4 cups vegetable stock

1/4 teaspoon of nutmeg

Olive oil

Salt and pepper to taste

1/2 cup toasted squash or pumpkin seeds, for garnish

Directions

1. Pre-heat the cooker by pressing the Sauté button. When hot, add the onions, sage, salt and pepper. When onions are soft, remove and set aside.

2. Add some squash cubes to cover the bottom of the pot, brown about 5 minutes stirring occasionally. Add the remaining squash, nutmeg, stock and ginger.

3. Seal lid, press Manual and select 10 minutes of cooking time. When beep sounds, open and quick release.

4. Remove the woody sage stem. Puree the contents of the cooker with a blend. Serve garnished with toasted pumpkin seeds.

Soy Curl Black Bean Feijoada

This dish can be made hot and spicy, if you like, by simply adding hot peppers. And if you would like to add salt, do so moments before serving. Bon Appétit!

Prep Time: 20minutes

Cook Time: 8hours

Waiting Time: 8hours

Servings: 10

Ingredients

5 cups black beans, dry

2 tablespoons granulated garlic powder

4 tablespoons granulated onion or onion powder

2 tablespoons freshly ground cumin powder

2 tablespoons oregano, dried and crushed

1 tablespoon turmeric powder or fresh

5 teaspoons bay leaves whole

4 ounces of Soy Curls

Directions

1. Sort beans and soak in plenty of water over-night or during the day for 8-12 hours.

2. Rinse beans well, put in the Instant-Pot and fill the liner to the maximum fill line.

3. Add all the seasoning ingredients except the soy curls. Set Instant-Pot to Slow Cook for 6 to 18 hours while you sleep, work or play!

4. 1 hour before serving, open the pressure cooker and add the soy curls. Reset Instant-Pot to Slow Cook again for 20-30 minutes.

Roast Baby Potatoes

Servings: 4-6.

Ingredients

2 lbs baby or fingerling potatoes

3 garlic cloves (outer skin on)

5 tablespoons of vegetable oil

1 cup stock

1 rosemary sprig

Salt and pepper to taste

Directions

1. Press Sauté to pre-heat the pressure cooker. When "Hot", add the vegetable oil, potatoes, rosemary and garlic. Swirl potatoes around and brown 8-10 minutes on all sides.

2. Pierce each potato in the middle with a sharp knife. Pour in the stock. Lock lid into place, press the Manual button and choose 11 minutes of cooking time.

3. When beep sounds, quick release by pressing cancel and twisting the steam release handle on the lid to the venting position.

4. Remove the garlic cloves' outer skin. Serve smashed or whole. Add salt and pepper to taste.

Split Pea Vegan Soup

A delicious, nutritious, and easy vegan recipe for you to enjoy.

Cook Time: 7minutes

Total Time: 7minutes

Servings: 4

Ingredients

1 lb carrots sliced

1 lb split beans (green and yellow, 1 cup each)

1bunch celery, sliced

1 large onion, chopped

4 cloves garlic minced

1½ teaspoon basil

1½ tsp oregano

1½ tsp celery seed

1½ tsp smoked paprika

4 teaspoon parsley flakes

4 Roma tomatoes, finely chopped

1 bag dried mushrooms

1 bay leaf

8 cups boiling water

Directions

1. Add all the ingredients to the Instant Pot.

2. Add water to the maximum point and bring to pressure for 6-7 minutes. Naturally release pressure.

3. Ladle the soup with kale, spinach, collards or other raw greens. The heat of the soup will cook the greens perfectly.

Easy Creamy Mashed Cauliflower
Creamy mashed cauliflower is easy to make and taste great.

Cook Time: 10 minutes

Servings: 2

Ingredients

Medium head of cauliflower, cut into smaller pieces, leaves and stem removed and the rest cut into sections of florets

2 cloves garlic

1/2 cup unsweetened almond milk

3tablespoons of nutritional yeast

1/2 teaspoon of freshly ground black pepper

1/2 teaspoon salt

1 cup water

Directions

1. Put the trivet in the Instant Pot and pour the water in. Add the cauliflower, cover, select "Steam" and set 3 minutes of cooking.

2. When program is completed, quick release pressure. Remove the cauliflower and blend in the blender.

3. Add the remaining ingredients and blend till the cauliflower is homogenized, soft and pliable.

Old- School Calico Beans
Ingredients:

1 pound bacon or bacon pieces

1 pound ground beef

1 large can of pork and beans

1 large onion, chopped

2, 15 ½-oz cans of kidney beans, drained

2, 15 ½- oz. cans of butter beans, drained

3 cups stewed tomatoes

½ cup sugar

1 cup corn

¾ cup brown sugar

½ cup ketchup

1 teaspoon mustard

3 tablespoons cider vinegar

1 teaspoon garlic, ground or chopped

1 tablespoon liquid smoke

Directions

1. Brown bacon in instant pot using the sauté setting; break it down and save drippings.

2. Add the hamburger & onion and brown, draining off excess fat.

3. Combine all ingredients, (drippings included) in the Instant Pot. Cook on manual setting for 25 minutes.

SOUPS AND STEWS

Beef Stew in Instant Pot

Servings: 4

Ingredients:

2 pounds beef stew meat

2 packets Stew Seasoning (I use McCormick)

5 scrubbed medium-sized potatoes, chopped

1 onion chopped

1 cup raw green beans

4 stalks celery

4 cups water

1 cup carrots chopped

Directions:

1. Add the beef stew meat, water and your preferred stew seasonings to the Instant Pot, seal lid and set valve into pressure (secure) position.

2. Select Manual mode on high pressure and set timer for 45-minutes. Wait 10-minutes then release pressure with valve. Uncover and stir.

3. Add all the vegetables, seal lid and secure valve to pressure. Select manual again and cook for 15 minutes. Wait 10 minutes. Release pressure.

Red Lentil Chili

So easy and delicious, this chili goes well with a baked sweet or white potato and topped with faux parmesan.

Prep Time: 15 Minutes

Cook Time: 20 Minutes

Total Time: 35 Minutes

Ingredients

1 pound red lentils

2 14.5 ounce cans diced tomatoes (preferably fire roasted)

1 6 ounce can tomato paste

10 ounces or 1 large chopped onion

3 ounces pitted dates

1 pound or 2large red bell peppers

8 cloves garlic, finely minced

4 tablespoons apple cider vinegar

1½ tablespoons of parsley flakes

1½ tablespoons of oregano

1½ tablespoons of chili powder

½(or more) teaspoon of chipotle powder

¼ teaspoon plus more of red pepper flakes, crushed

7 cups of water, divided

2 teaspoon paprika (smoked, preferred)

Directions

1. In a blender, blend the red bell pepper, dates, tomatoes, one cup water and garlic until smooth.

2. Place remaining ingredients, including the date mixture, in the pressure cooker and cook10 minutes on high.

3. Let pressure release naturally, and enjoy with baked potato and parmesan.

Texas Trail Chili
Servings: 8

Ingredients:

1-1/2 pounds of ground beef, chicken or turkey

2 tablespoons canola oil

2 cups favorite Bloody Mary mix

1 large onion, peeled & chopped

2 Cans (14 ounces each) kidney beans, drained & rinsed well

1- 28-ounce can diced tomatoes with juice or 2 Cans (14 ounces each) diced tomatoes with green chilies

4 tablespoons chili powder, divided

1-1/2 cups of water

Directions

1. Heat oil in instant pot and add the onion, sautéing 8-10 minutes until lightly brown.

2. Add the meat, cook until browns, breaking it up while it cooks. Add the Bloody Mary mix, heat on medium-high and stir.

3. Add the beans, 2 tablespoons of chili powder and tomatoes. Stir and bring to a boil and then add the water.

4. Secure lid and cook 5 minutes on high pressure. Quick release steam and remove the lid when the pressure valve drops.

5. Add more tablespoons chili powder, stir and let it stand for 5 minutes.

6. Serve and garnish with shredded cheese, sour cream, corn ships or sliced green onions or as desired.

Instant Pot Chinese Beef Stew

Prep Time: 12 minutes

Cook Time: 30 minutes

Servings: 4-6

Ingredients:

2 lb beef round, cut into one inch pieces

1-2 tablespoons of oil

1-2 teaspoons fresh ginger, finely chopped

2 teaspoons sherry or rice wine

2 medium onions sliced

1 tablespoon soy sauce

½ tsp sugar

2 teaspoons cornstarch

½ cup broth, preferably beef

1 tablespoon Worcestershire sauce

Pinch of smoked Paprika

1-2 teaspoon cornstarch slurry (optional)

1 can of mushrooms (optional)

1-2 garlic powder (to taste)

Salt and pepper

Directions

1. Sauté onions until just translucent. Add rice wine, soy sauce and sugar and stir fry 30 seconds. Add beef in dry ingredients, add to pot, stir and stir fry 30 seconds. Stir in the beef broth and Worcestershire sauce and secure lid.

2. Set on soup mode for 30 minutes, keep warm 3 minutes and release pressure. Check the meat for moisture and doneness and set to "Stew" for 2-4 more minutes.

3. When done, add ginger, mushrooms (if using) and salt and pepper (if needed). Thicken to desired taste by adding cornstarch slurry (if needed).

4. Sauté 1 minute. Serve with rice and sautéed greens or freshly cut veggies.

Adzuki Bean Soup

Enjoy this popular Asian after dinner-dessert recipe prepared in just 1 hour!

Prep Time: 5 minutes

Cook Time: 55 minutes

Servings: 6

Ingredients

2 cups red beans

1/2 cup dry lotus seeds, sprouts removed

4 tablespoon sugar

1/2 cup dry chestnuts, optional

2 small pieces of dried lemon peel or mandarin, broken into tiny pieces, optional

8-12 cups water (depending on how thick or thin you want your soup)

Directions

1. Put all the ingredients in the pressure cooker

2. Select "Bean/Chilli" function and press "Adjust" once to set the cooking time.

2. Once done, stir well and serve.

Easy Breezy Chunky Chicken And Veggie Soup
Yummy!

Servings: 2-4

Ingredients

1 lb frozen chicken breasts (3 to 4)

2 squash or zucchini, chopped chunky

2 medium potatoes, skin-on, quartered

1 onion quartered

1 stalk celery, chopped chunky

1 carrot, chopped chunky

2 teaspoon diced garlic

1 tablespoon of Italian Seasoning

1 can of Progresso Parmesan Recipe Starters

1 tablespoon of ground flaxseed (optional)

Salt & Pepper to taste

Directions

1. Put all the ingredients in the Instant Pot except for salt and pepper. Stir to combine. Close lid, push the rice button and set 12 minutes. Let pressure release naturally

2. Remove lid. Shred chicken breasts with two forks. Stir soup gently and season with salt and pepper.

3. Replace lid and set to "keep warm" for 30 minutes to integrate the flavor in the poultry. Serve with whole grain roll, freshly baked.

Winter Spicy Veggie Soup

This dish is a treat, especially during the winter season. Don't you just love its spiciness?

Servings: 2-3

Ingredients

1 cup celery, chopped

1 medium onion, chopped

1/2 cup carrots, chopped

1 fresh jalapeno (3inch long), chopped, with membrane &seeds removed

2 tbsp olive oil

1/2 tsp cumin seed

1 tsp coriander seeds

3 big russet potatoes, cubed, with peels on

2 ½ -3 quarts low sodium chicken broth

2 tablespoon chicken broth

4 cups water

1 tsp. ground cumin

1/4 tsp ground turmeric

2 tablespoon pickled jalapenos, chopped

Chopped cilantro to taste

Directions

1. Set Instant Pot on Sauté. Add olive oil and let it warm up for about 1 minute.

2. Add cumin seeds and coriander seeds and heat until the coriander seeds pop. Add the chopped carrots, celery, jalapeno and onion. Sauté about 5 minutes until onions are translucent.

3. Add the turmeric, pickled jalapenos and cumin. Add the potatoes and chicken broth. Set to soup position for 30 minutes. Let pressure release normally.

4. Add the chopped cilantro just before serving. Serve with good bread.

Open Country Clam Chowder

Servings: 4 -6

Ingredients

2 cups clam juice (or use liquid from packaged clams and water)

11 oz strained frozen or canned clams

1 cup, smoked & cured bacon cubed

1 onion, thinly chopped

1/2 cup white wine

2 medium potatoes, cubed

1 sprig thyme

1 pinch, red pepper flakes or cayenne pepper

1 cup of cream

1 cup of milk

1 tablespoons of butter

1 tablespoons of flour

1 bay leaf

Directions

1. Place bacon in the Instant Pot and press sauté button and adjust until it is 'Less'. When the bacon starts to sizzle, add the onion, pepper and salt. Press cancel to raise the heat then press the sauté button again.

2. When the onions soften, add the wine, scraping any brown bits off the bottom of the pot to add into your sauce. Once the wine evaporates, add the potatoes, cayenne pepper, clam juice, thyme and bay leaf.

3. Lock lid into place. Press 'manual' and set 5 minutes of cooking time. When beep sounds, open lid and quick release.

4. Meanwhile, prepare the roux to thicken the chowder. Blend equal amounts of flour and butter over low heat and stir often until well mixed.

5. Add the roux, strained clams, milk and cream to the Instant pot. Press Sauté and simmer all the contents of the Instant Pot until thickened as preferred.

6. Serve with soup crackers or bread.

Rich Oxtails Stew

Prep Time: 5 minutes

Cook Time: 50 minutes

Ingredients:

5 lbs oxtails

2 cups red wine

1 large onion, peeled & chopped

3 stalks celery, chopped

3 carrots, chopped

1 cup chopped tomatoes

1 small bunch parsley, chopped

1 clove garlic, peeled and chopped

1 cup water

Sugar to taste

Salt and pepper

Directions

1. Season the oxtails with salt and pepper and place in the pressure cooker.

2. Place the remaining ingredients, except the wine and water on top of the oxtails. Now pour the wine and water over all items.

3. Cook for 40minutes at stew setting. Let warm in the pot for 10minutes before opening the lid.

4. Season with salt, pepper, serve and enjoy.

One Pot Beef Bone Broth

This recipe can also be set to Slow Cooker and cook 16 to 24 hours on low.

Prep Time: 5 minutes

Cook Time: 2 hours

Total Time: 2 hours 5 minutes

Serving: 6-8 cups

Ingredients

3 pounds beef soup bones (plus two knuckle bones)

6 cloves garlic, peeled

3 stalks celery, washed & cut in two

4 large carrots, washed & cut in two

1 medium onion, cut into quarters

1 tablespoon apple cider vinegar

1 tablespoon kosher salt

6-8 cups of filtered Water (do not exceed the Instant Pot's fill line)

Directions

1. Place all the ingredients in the Instant Pot. Lock lid in place. Set vent to seal position.

2. Set to "Soup", set timer to 120 minutes. Once done, turn on or leave on "Warm". Let pressure release and open lid.

3. Remove vegetables and bones with a slotted spoon and pass broth through a strainer. Enjoy!

Soothing Soup Potato

Cook Time: 30 minutes

Makes 8 cups

Ingredients

1/2 teaspoon olive oil

2 slices bacon

1 onion, diced

1 cup of low sodium chicken broth

1 teaspoon minced garlic

2 1/2 lbs potatoes, peeled & chopped into 1- inch cubes

2 carrots, diced

1 tablespoon dried parsley

12 ounce can of evaporated milk

1 celery stalk, diced

2 cups of low sodium chicken broth

1 teaspoon dried Italian Seasoning

1 ½ teaspoons salt, to taste

Black pepper to taste

Dash of dried red pepper flakes

Directions

1. Press Sauté on Instant Pot. Add olive oil, onion, garlic and bacon. Stir while sautéing 3-4 minutes.

2. Add 1 cup chicken broth, carrots, potatoes, red pepper flakes, celery, parsley and Italian seasoning. Stir. Secure lid, press the steam button and set to 10 minutes. Quick- release pressure.

3. Remove the bacon and discard. Now add 2 cups of chicken broth and evaporated milk. Puree with an emersion blender until desired creamy consistency is attained but leave chunks of potatoes.

4. Season with salt and pepper and stir to incorporate.

Tasty Chowder With Potato& Bacon

This tasty Potato Bacon Chowder is so simple and remarkably fast. Just 5 minutes of actual cooking time!

Servings: 8

Ingredients

1 large onion, small diced

5 lbs. russet potatoes, peeled & cubed

1 lb. bacon, crisply fried & chopped rough

3 stalks celery, thinly sliced

4 cups chicken stock

1 clove garlic, minced

1 teaspoon ground black pepper

1 tablespoon seasoning salt

1 cup heavy cream

½ cup whole milk

¼ cup of butter

Sour cream, diced green onion and shredded cheddar cheese (for garnish)

Directions

1. Place the potato chunks in the Instant Pot. Add onion, celery, garlic, butter, salt and pepper, stirring to combine.

2. Add chicken stock and bacon to pot and stir. Secure lid on the Instant Pot slow cooker, press button to "Manual" and set timer to 5 minutes. Quickly release pressure.

3. Once steam is completely gone, remove the lid. Crush vegetables with a potato masher until it is a thick semi-smooth mash.

4. Add whole milk and cream, stir well. Serve topped with sour cream, sliced green onion and shredded cheddar.

Broccoli Beef Soup & Kelp Noodles
Cook Time: 50 minutes

Servings: 8

Ingredients

4 cups beef bone broth

2 tablespoons sesame oil

2 carrots, peeled and diced

1 teaspoon sea salt

2 pounds of grass fed beef stew meat, cut into cubes of1 inch

2 celery stalks, diced

1 onion, diced

5 cloves garlic, minced

½ cup dry sherry

3 tablespoons minced fresh ginger

¼ cup soy sauce or coconut aminos

2 heads broccoli, flowerets cut small, stemmed, peeled & diced

2 packages Sea Tangle Kelp Noodles

½ of a small savory cabbage, chiffonade

Sriracha to taste

Chopped cilantro for garnish

½ teaspoon fresh ground pepper

Directions

1. Set Instant Pot to Sauté. Add Sesame oil. Season meat with salt and pepper and add to pot. Cook, and turn until well browned for about 5 minutes. Remove meat to a plate and then set aside.

2. Add the carrots, onion and celery and cook, about 3 minutes, stirring until the veggies are wilted.

3. Add the meat, ginger, garlic, broth, coconut aminos and sherry. Cover and cook 20 minutes.

4. Add the cabbage and broccoli, stir thoroughly, and replace lid. Cook 20 more minutes.

5. Garnish with cilantro and enjoy with Kelp noodles and sriracha.

Tofu &Winter Melon Soup

Meal type: Pork

Prep Time: 10 minutes

Cook Time: 45minutes

Stand Time: 24 hours

Servings: 6

Ingredients

1 lb Pork bones

5 cups water

1 package tofu 700g

1¾ lb. Winter melon

1 tablespoon olive oil

1 tablespoon green onion, chopped

2-3 slices of fresh ginger

2 cilantro rinsed & chopped

1/4 teaspoon ground black pepper

2 teaspoon salt

Directions

1. Place tofu in freezer overnight. Soak the pork bones with boiling water for 3-4 minutes, drain, wash and rinse pork bones with cold water.

2. Place the pork bones inside the pressure cooker and add 5 cups of cold water. Cover lid and set pressure valve to "Seal" position. Hit the "Manual" button and set cooking time 35 minutes.

3. When done, wait 5 minutes more. Release the pressure slowly, and then open the lid. Once the pork stock cools, place lid on the inner pot and refrigerate.

4. Defrost frozen tofu the next day. Peel off winter melon skin, rinse and slice. Cut defrost tofu into small pieces.

5. In a non-stick pan, heat olive oil, sauté ginger and chopped green onion 1 minute, add the sliced winter melon and tofu, stir and cook 3-4 minutes.

6. Skim fat off of pork and then pour stock into the winter melon and tofu, bring to boil. Lower heat; add salt and black pepper and simmer until winter melon softens, that will be about15 minutes.

7. Divide soup into 6 bowls, scatter chopped cilantro over them and serve.

Dry Split Pea Soup

Total Time: 1hour

Servings: 6

Ingredients

1 onion, chopped

2 cups dry split peas

3 stalks celery, diced

1 Rapunzel vegetable bouillon cube, herbs included

1 teaspoon extra virgin olive oil (to stop peas from foaming and clogging up the Instant Pot)

1/2 teaspoon granulated garlic

1/4 teaspoon black pepper

1 bay leaf

2 carrots, peeled& shredded coarsely

8 cups hot water

1 or 2 tablespoons of fresh lemon juice (optional)

Salt to taste

Directions

1. Remove dirt or small rocks from the split peas, place them in a strainer and then rinse well.

2. Place the split peas in the pressure cooker and add all the ingredients except the carrots. Stir to let the bouillon cube mix well with the hot water.

3. Secure lid and ensure top vent is closed. Press 'manual' on the button and set 12 minutes. When done, release pressure naturally and then remove lid cautiously.

4. Taste for seasonings; add salt and black pepper if necessary. Also, if needed, add 1-2 tablespoon freshly squeezed lemon juice to the soup to brighten the taste. Soup will thicken as it cools.

RICE & PASTA RECIPES

One Pot Basmati Rice

Servings: 4

Ingredients

2 cups of Basmati Rice

3 cups of Water

Directions

1. Rinse the rice in a strainer, cover and soak in fresh water for 15 minutes.

2. Strain rice; add to the Instant Pot and add water. Secure lid, press the manual function and choose 4 minutes of cooking time.

3. When the program ends, wait 10 minutes then natural release pressure by pressing cancel and twisting the steam release handle to the "Venting" position.

One Pot Jasmine Rice
Servings: 4-6

Ingredients

2 cups of Jasmine Rice

3 cups of Water

Directions

1. Rinse the rice in a strainer, cover and soak in fresh water for 15 minutes.

2. Strain rice; add to the Instant Pot and add water. Secure lid, press the manual function and choose 4 minutes of cooking time.

3. When the program ends, wait 10 minutes then natural release pressure by pressing cancel and twisting the steam release handle to the "Venting" position.

One Pot Brown Rice
Servings: 4

Ingredients

2 cups of Brown Rice

2 ½ cups of Water

Directions

1. Rinse the rice in a strainer, cover and soak in fresh water for 15 minutes.

2. Strain rice; add to the Instant Pot and add water. Secure lid, press the manual function and choose 22 minutes of cooking time.

3. When the program ends, wait 10 minutes then natural release pressure by pressing cancel and twisting the steam release handle to the "Venting" position

Multigrain Rice

Whole grains contain lots of nutrients and fiber and are low in fat. Consuming whole grains helps in the significant reduction of heart diseases and type II diabetes. Multiple grains can be combined to create a large variety of wholegrain meal. They hardly overcook and pleasantly retain their texture after cooking.

Prep Time: 2 minutes

Cook Time: 70 minutes

Servings: 6-8

Ingredients

3 cups of grains such as wild rice and brown rice

2 tablespoon of olive oil

3¾ – 4 ½ cups of water

1 ½ teaspoon salt, optional

Directions

1. Add together the grains, oil, water and salt, if using, in the Instant Pot.

2. Select the Multigrain function and when the program ends, wait for 5 minutes before opening the lid.

3. Stir and serve.

Coconut Mango Arborio Rice Pudding

Ingredients:

3/4 cup Arborio Rice

1 mango, peeled and cubed

1 can light coconut milk

1/3 cup brown sugar

1/2 cup half and half

1 1/2 cups water

1 tsp vanilla

1 tsp salt

1/4 cup shredded coconut, pulsed (for garnish)

1/4 cup of almonds, pulsed (for garnish)

Directions

1. Add rice, coconut milk, sugar, salt and water to the pressure cooker. Set on manual and set time to 7 minutes at High pressure.

2. Use natural release. Unlock lid and uncover rice.

3. Add in vanilla, chopped mango and half and half. Stir and serve in bowls with toasted almonds and coconut over top.

Instant Pot Pasta

To prevent sogginess, be sure to add just the right amount of liquid to your pasta.

Prep Time: 5 minutes

Cook Time: 35 minutes

Ingredients:

1 pound (1 box) Penne pasta, uncooked

2 lbs of ground meat

3 cups of chicken broth

2 small cans of sliced mushrooms

1 large sweet onion, finely chopped

2 cloves minced garlic

2 cups mozzarella cheese, shredded

2 tablespoons olive oil

2 tbsp Italian Seasoning

1/4 tsp. red pepper flakes

45 oz. (1 jar) spaghetti sauce

1 cup red wine

1 teaspoon salt

1/2 teaspoon black pepper

Directions:

1. Sauté the onion and garlic in the olive oil on the browning setting on your Instant Pot.

2. Add the ground meat and brown. Add the pasta, mushrooms with liquid, wine, chicken broth to cover the pasta, sauces and all the seasonings. Secure lid, set to meat mode and cook 20 minutes.

3. Manually release pressure. Stir and add mozzarella cheese. Leave for 10 minutes. Serve and enjoy.

Bow Tie Pasta In The Pressure Cooker

Enjoy this quick, easy and tasty meal – it's just perfect for a weeknight meal!

Ingredients

16 oz. Bow-Tie Pasta

1 pound lean ground sausage (or chicken sausage)

1 tablespoon of olive oil

1 onion, finely chopped

28 oz. can crushed tomatoes in puree

2 cloves garlic, crushed

1 teaspoon of dried basil

1/4 teaspoon of salt

1/8 teaspoon of red pepper flakes

3 ½ cups of water

Directions

1. Add olive oil to pot, select sauté or browning. When the oil starts to sizzle, add garlic, onion and sausage and sauté about 10 minutes until onion is tender and meat loses its pinkness.

2. Add the rest of the ingredients and stir. Select high pressure, set for 5 minutes. Quick release pressure and when the valve drops, remove lid carefully.

3. Stir mixture. Select simmer and cook, 2 to 5 minutes, stirring constantly, until the pasta is tender. Season with salt and pepper.

Pineapple And Cauliflower Mixed Rice

Every kid will love this pineapple and veggie mixed rice because of its pleasant aroma and delicious taste.

Prep Time: 5 minutes

Cook Time: 30minutes

Servings: 6

Ingredients

2 cups rice

1 cauliflower minced

1/2 pineapple or ½ can pineapple, minced

1 teaspoon salt

2 teaspoons oil

Directions

1. Add water to the instant pot to fill the level 2 mark. (The required amount of water depends on the type of rice, though).

2. Add all ingredients and then press the rice button. Once done, serve and enjoy.

Rice With Sausage And Potato

Fast, easy and convenient, this one-pot dish is for everyone.

Prep Time: 15 minutes

Cook Time: 20 minutes

Servings: 8

Ingredients

2 cups of long grain rice

2 lean Chinese sausages cut thinly into slices

1½ tbsp olive oil

5 small yellow potatoes (400g), peeled & cut into small pieces

1½ tablespoon green onion, finely chopped

3-4 slices of fresh ginger

1¼ tsp salt

3 cups water

¼ tsp chicken broth mix

1/6 teaspoon ground black pepper

1 tbsp green onion, finely chopped

Directions

1. Rinse sausages and potatoes under cold water; drain. Add olive oil to Instant Pot, press the "Sauté" button then "Adjust" to set temperature to "More".

2. Sauté green onion and ginger for 2-4 minutes. Add sausages and cook 1-2 minutes. Add potatoes and cook 1-2 more minutes.

3. Add rice and combine thoroughly. Add 2 long grain rice, salt, ground black pepper, water and chicken broth mix. Secure lid and place pressure valve to "Seal" position and press "Rice".

4. Once program is done, hold on for another 5minutes and release the pressure slowly then open the lid.

5. Add a tablespoon of chopped green onion, mix thoroughly and then serve.

Mediterranean Tuna Noodle Delight

Ingredients:

8 oz dry wide egg noodles

1 can tuna fish in water, drained

1 tablespoon of oil

1 can (14 oz) diced tomatoes with garlic, basil, and oregano (un-drained)

½ cup of chopped red onion

¼ teaspoon of salt

1 jar (7.5 oz.) marinated artichoke hearts, drained with liquid saved, then chopped up.

1-1/4 cups of water

Crumpled feta cheese

Fresh or dried parsley, chopped

1/8 teaspoon pepper

Directions:

1. In the Instant Pot, sauté red onion 2-3 minutes. Add the tomatoes, dry noodles, salt, pepper and water. Cook on soup mode for 10 minutes. Release the pressure valve and turn off warm setting.

2. Add artichokes, tuna, and the reserved artichokes liquid, sauté on normal and stir continuously until hot.

3. Top with feta cheese and parsley.

MISCELLANEOUS RECIPES

Steamed Fresh Corn

Steam your corn in just 12 minutes. Could any kitchenware be better than the Instant Pot?

Prep Time: 5 minutes

Cook Time: 12 minutes

Servings: 6

Ingredients

6 fresh corns

Directions

1. Husk the corns and rinse them.

2. Place the steam rack inside pressure cooker. Pour water till it reaches its 2-cup mark. Stack the corns on the steam rack and secure lid.

3. Turn the valve to the Seal position. Select the "Steam" button and set timer to 12 minutes to cook.

4. Once it is cooked, wait 5 more minutes. Release the pressure slowly and then open the lid. Remove the steamed corns and enjoy.

Purple Yam Pearl Barley Porridge

Purple yam is loaded with anti-oxidants and high in fiber. Its purplish color makes exceptional exotic porridge.

Prep Time: 10 minutes

Cook time: 45 minutes

Servings: 12

Ingredients:

1 purple yam (about 300g)

3 tablespoons pearl barley

3 tablespoons pot barley

3 tablespoons buckwheat

3 tablespoons glutinous rice

3 tablespoons black glutinous rice

3 tablespoons black eye beans

3 tablespoons red beans

3 tablespoons Romano beans

3 tablespoons brown rice

1/6 tsp baking soda (optional)

Directions:

1. Clean yam, remove skin and cut into1cm cubes. Wash the rice, beans and barley in the Instant Pot.

2. Place the yam cubes and the baking soda in it and fill water to the 8 mark. Close the lid, set steam release to the seal position. Set Congee mode and adjust cooking time to 45 minutes.

4. After the program ends, cool 10 minutes. Serve plain or with blue agave syrup, sugar or honey.

Mashed Potatoes With Greek Yogurt
A healthy and delicious mashed potato recipe for the family

Servings: 4

Ingredients

1 ½ pounds peeled baking potatoes (about 3 medium-sized)

1/2 tablespoon butter

1/2 cup skim milk

1/2 teaspoon minced garlic

1/2 cup whole milk Greek yogurt

1/2 cup water

Salt, to taste

Dashes of pepper, to taste

Grated cheddar cheese for garnish, optional

Directions

1. Pour water in the Instant Pot. Place the potatoes on top of the trivet and secure lid. Press the steam button and then set timer to 35 minutes.

2. When cooking program is completed, do a quick release, and remove lid. Confirm softness by inserting a fork in the largest potato otherwise steam another 3-5 minutes.

3. Turn off Instant Pot. Use tongs or a fork to remove the hot trivet. Add the yogurt, butter, garlic and half of the skim milk. Insert a potato masher and mash to desired consistency. Season with salt and pepper.

4. Remove the mashed potatoes to a bowl and garnish with grated cheese.

Fish With Beer & Potato

With your instant pot, this delicious but challenging recipe for beginners is now easy to prepare.

Prep Time: 15 minutes

Cook Time: 40 minutes

Servings: 6

Ingredients:

1 pound fish fillet

1 cup beer

1 tablespoon oyster flavored sauce

4 medium size potatoes, peeled and diced

1 tablespoon oil

1 red pepper sliced

1 tablespoon of rock candy

1 teaspoon salt

Directions

1. Put all the ingredients in the Instant Pot and press the Bean/Chili button.

2. When program ends, do a natural release. Serve and enjoy.

Taro Sausage Cake

Taro is a highly nutritious root vegetable that can be cooked like potato. It contains vitamin C, E and Bs, potassium, calcium and magnesium and also helps to prevent diabetes.

Prep Time: 25 minutes

Cook time: 55 minutes

Servings: 10

Ingredients

1 large (500 g) taro root, peeled & shred

1 ½ Chinese sausages cut into pieces

2 tablespoon of dried shrimp (soaked in warm water, strained & cut into pieces)

1 tablespoon olive oil

1 tsp minced ginger

3 tablespoon green onion, finely chopped

11/3 teaspoon salt, divided

1/2 teaspoon of sugar

¼ teaspoon of chicken broth mix

11/3 cups rice flour

2 cups water

3 tablespoons of olive oil

Directions

1. Add a tablespoon of olive oil to a non-stick pan, sauté ginger and green onion on medium-high heat setting for 1 minute.

2. Add dried shrimp and sausage, cook1 minute more. Add taro root and cook for 1 or 2 minutes. Add salt, sugar and chicken broth mix and cook 2 minutes. Set aside to cool.

3. Combine rice flour and water in a bowl. Pour into the taro pan and mix thoroughly. Pour the batter into glass container

4. In the Instant Pot, fill water to 2-cup mark and then place the glass container on the steam rack inside the pressure cooker.

5. Cover lid, turn the pressure valve to "Seal" and press the "Steam" button. Set the cooking time to 40 minutes. Once done, wait 10 minutes, release pressure slowly, and then open the lid.

6. Remove the steamed taro cake; set aside to cool. Cover and refrigerate a few hours. Loosen the taro cake along the edges. Turn the glass container upside down, pry taro cake out and slice into 4 mm thickness

7. In a non-stick pan, heat a tablespoon olive oil over medium heat. Stir- fry 1/3 of taro cake until light brown on both sides. Remove to a platter and serve.

The End

46638946R00089

Made in the USA
Lexington, KY
11 November 2015